CORONAVIRUS
and the Strange Death of Truth

by

Brian Patrick Bolger

Grosvenor House
Publishing Limited

This book is published by
Grosvenor House Publishing Ltd
Link House
140 The Broadway, Tolworth, Surrey, KT6 7HT.
www.grosvenorhousepublishing.co.uk

A CIP record for this book
is available from the British Library

ISBN 978-1-83975-622-1

Dedication

For my wife Eva and my sons Oliver and Albert.

Acknowledgements

I would like to thank Professor Adrian Wilkinson, at Griffith University, Australia, for his part in helping me with structure and comments regarding the book, and the Publisher for working with me on the book.

Foreword:

An impressive wide-ranging and readable book covering History, Politics, Economics and Culture and tracing the ills of the Coronavirus to the unstable world created by Globalisation and Inequality. Bolger provides insightful commentary and argues that change is possible, and we should use the current crisis to reconnect and recognise the importance of solidarity and cooperation.

Professor Adrian Wilkinson,
Griffith University, Australia

Contents

Part 2: The Strange Death of Truth

Preface

The book evolved from an original critique of contemporary society, of which I had some ideas, into a full-blown book idea once the Coronavirus episode began to unfold in 2020. The ideas within the book do not fall into established notions such as left and right; in fact, the book calls for a syncretism and synthesis of ideas into a new movement to replace these old models. It appeared more and more that the Coronavirus was merely one aspect of a greater, inter-related crisis which was unfolding. The synthesis is the book as it appears now: 'Coronavirus and the Strange Death of Truth'. The original title 'Coronavirus and the Real Cost of Globalisation' is to be published in the US.

Coronavirus and the Strange Death of Truth

'The present age prefers the sign to the thing signified, the copy to the original, fancy to reality, the appearance to the essence for in these days illusion only is sacred, truth profane.'

Ludwig Feuerbach, *The Essence of Christianity*. 1841.[1]

Introduction

The book is a contemporary painting of modern society akin to Robert Frank's photography in *The Americans* or a walk through a Banksy 'exhibition'. Just as Frank's 'America' is more poetry than photography, this book is a picture book rather than a quantitative analysis. The Coronavirus illustrates the unstable world that globalisation has created; a dangerous dependency on global trade which previous generations had never known. The book outlines the contradictions inherent in neo-liberal Environment, Growth, Inequality, and Globalisation theories. The book shows the dangerous contractions of freedom and truth inherent in 'globalised' economies and structures. It paints a possible alternative based on 'degrowth' and localised economies. It discusses a return to a Westphalian system of nation statism based on respect and legitimacy. It critiques contemporary views on 'technology' and questions the 'progressive' mantra that economists and cultural observers place on technology.

The book proposes that Coronavirus and its deadly impact cannot be seen as an isolated issue which can be solved by medicine or money. Bill Gates, in 2015, said that the biggest threat to the world was not wars but germs. The greatest threat is the fundamental ontology of the West, which, increasingly, places nations on the precipice of war and plague. Therefore, the inherent contradictions of a society locked into the 'Military-Industrial-Technology' complex needs to be replaced by one which prepares civilisation for increasing problems linked to globalisation. It is symptomatic of a deeper malaise of economic, political, and cultural interconnectivity. The book analyses the neo-liberal take on the economic sphere and its roots in a change of 'telos' since the Enlightenment. So, whilst the Coronavirus has its contemporary roots in two problems – globalisation and inequality – the underlying moral teleological decline started with the

Enlightenment. It argues that liberal democracy does not offer solutions to cataclysmic impacts such as Coronavirus or the 2008 banking crisis. The final section looks at the decline in democracy in the 'Occident', and the related contraction of freedom and truth. The book can be taken as an allegory of a 'Plague'. The initial symptom is the manifestation of illness, but the real plague is something else completely – it is the plague of liberal cultural ideology.

The modern world exhibits a tension between tradition and freedom (in the sense of the autonomous individual of rationalism). The dilemma of modern capitalism is that it has unleashed the corollary of economic liberalism and the unfettered free market; this is 'negative freedom', which means unfettered individual behaviour not tempered by obligations. The world is awash with 'rights'; rights dominate discourse, and it is an especial ally for the liberal since they are able to 'dispense' rights. This absence of moral restraint is the corollary to economic freedom, and, understandably, leaves homo sapiens in a constant tension. The traditional world offered a realm of spiritual and teleological guidance; whilst the realms of economic freedoms remained only titular for many in pre-Enlightenment times. The post-industrial revolution world expected the working-class to exist in unfree servitude – both at work through 'planned economies', and at home, under the waning influence of the Church. The modern world, in a revolutionary thrust, now leaves these people in the arid desert lands: precarious work, and without any spiritual guidance or explanation for the vicissitudes of life. This tension has manifested itself in the confused state of people searching for meaning; the clash of discontents has been visible during the Coronavirus crisis. Plague brings human action under the microscope and magnifies the tension. The modern liberal fails to see that by rejecting tradition, they also reject the formative influences through millennia, which shape homo sapiens. This tension has existed since the Industrial Revolution and was played out, in various ways, between left and right. What is seminal now is the desecration of tradition and the iconoclastic liberal onslaught unfettered by knowledge.

Morality and virtue, however, are also determined by culture; there is a symbiotic tension and struggle. The solution is not the Nietzschean 'Superman' looking into himself, but the man of tradition and freedom. The march of the Leviathan of the State, hand-in-hand with prescriptive technology, has reduced the realms of traditional freedom even further; there is no balance, and the centre cannot hold. The origins of the current economic and existential threats lie in a deeper misalignment between the purposes of human life and the web of systems we have designed through history. Therefore, technological approaches or medical solutions are insufficient to address endemic issues. They are akin to fixing holes in the web. Likewise, a tampering of economic or cultural edifices will not repair the whole. The issues facing modernity need a recalibration of virtue and morality through a truthful dialogue; they need, moreover, to address why the human spider builds the web, why he acts as he does, and to what purpose, and should that be ethical. Virtue was shifted during the Enlightenment, from being based on an end purpose of life or teleology, to one based upon natural rights or utility. If we accept the premises of later belief systems of the nineteenth and twentieth centuries – the nihilism of Nietzsche or the 'choices' of Kierkegaard – then we are missing the origins of virtue, of the web. At the centre of the Enlightenment was the notion that homo sapiens faced a constant struggle between Hume's passion and Kantian reason. Aristotle's solution was that there is a purpose and an end point to act morally, and that was the end product of community. An individual had good reason to behave ethically as part of a 'recognisable' or felt community. Traditional man, moreover, saw his role outlined in this way.

However, the modern globalised world, the Leviathan of the State, sees the realms of work 'atomised' and detached from human existence and real community forgotten. Power relations are such that moral existence becomes more and more individual choice. The Enlightenment gave to humanity the open recourse to 'choice'. This was seen as a progressive force; the abandonment of attachments to family, church, and community, as the world of capital demanded the cutting of ties. The issue is that the values and edicts from this period are taken as *de rigeur* and accepted, the same way as the notion of 'rights' is dispensed as if at the shopping mall by the *traison de clercs* of modernity. Therefore, the choices become individualised, and this has been extended to the point where certain choices are available whilst others are demonised. Hence, we have an intellectual impasse whereby everything about modernity is my choice; children are free to choose their mode of learning, then the children can choose from a smorgasbord of sexual preferences, the choice of a baby's sex.

However, other values are not considered to be rightly chosen – for example, chastity or drug use – although there is no logic underpinning such a negation of those choices once you derive moral action based on *laissez faire* 'choice'. Hence there is an underlying confusion to the web modern man has created, as modernity has uprooted mankind from a community of shared consciousness. Therefore, true and false became illegitimate; hence the contradiction that x may be held by the majority to be right/ wrong, but it is seen as a mistake to think that x is right/wrong. Moral questions become akin to matters of taste, embedded in a web of consumerism. Consequently, the impasse is the strange death of truth, which can only be resolved by recourse to a fundamental reform of social structures, on the one hand, and a moral teleological rebirth.

The technical autocratic phase of liberal democracy was not a great surprise to those on the left or those on the right. It wasn't a phase in the sense of a Hegelian or Marxian inevitability, what Philosophers call Historicism. It was merely part of the necessity to squeeze ordinary people in the move to a technical version of capitalism. Huge, indebted economies were a means to extend capital amongst elites, through cheap money and government bonds. The apparatus of government has been infiltrated by accumulative elites akin to a type of gangster capitalism. This can be seen in the oligarchic model in Russia and the privatisation of the public sector in the UK. The problem is that the people in the middle, the stalwarts of liberal democracy, have been co-opted into the system through an inflated public sector, at home, in the EU, and through global governance. Government is now run by pushing the borders of tolerance; a behaviourist plan is behind the push out of the Coronavirus strategy, therefore an organisation like Sage employs behavioural psychologists to set the public response to the pandemic, to 'frame' the issues to elicit the response necessary to manage tolerance. This clever behaviourist strategy works in China and has been implemented gradually in European liberal democracies.

An authoritarian society employs a technological apparatus to, ostensibly, deliver solutions. However, it is elites which set the questions and frame the responses. With the Coronavirus response, that is a computer modelling system rolled out without public consultation or debate, without peer review. Likewise, the lockdown was implemented with a disdain for civil liberties or freedom, again without public consultation. Behavioural manipulation is then used, through the media and social media, to 'manage' the public's response. The technological presentation ensures the policy appears neutral; in fact, lockdown success depends on the 'performance' of the public, about their correct distancing, masking. Any alternative, such as studying past pandemics or the advice of virologists, is presented as 'unscientific'. Lockdowns are non-medical interventions; they are not part of medical science. They are a continuation and development away from participatory models of democracy and liberty. Yet the UK government presents the use of expert data and modelling as the only method. The 'model' causes x, y, and z problems through lockdown, but the government can hide behind the inevitable consequences. However, these consequences have nothing to do with the virus; they are the economic costs, the suicides, depression, etc, of the lockdown. Coronavirus and lockdown, however, are not a sudden fancy on the part of the Western elites. The squeezing of democracy, freedom, and national identities has been a gradual process, worked out through extra-democratic means from the inculcation of liberal education systems and a gradual dismemberment of freedoms through legislation. In 1978 Alexander Solzhenitsyn gave his commencement address at Harvard. He noted the tidal ebbing away of courage in the West; he said we should fear this more than death. He noted that 'safety and well-being are not advantageous to a living organism'. The tide of courage which he saw decimated in the West has now ended in a stagnant pool of liberal sentiments, the feminisation of society, and a liberal world view based on atomised, soulless individuals, praying to the god of technology. The Occident has given up its ontology based on spirit and community and sold their soul to Mephistopheles for the comfortable soporific of liberalism.

PART 1
Coronavirus and Globalisation

Coronavirus and Globalisation

The Enlightenment is dead. The Cold War saw the eclipse of the Soviet Union by the US in a period of industrial competition. The war was won, not through the might of the US military machine, but through the inconsistencies within a planned economy. The new Cold War between the US and China assumes that the Leviathan of China, despite its technological prowess, will succumb to the contradictions of its own internal system; a Leninist executive within a market-like economy. However, just like the Industrial Revolution fomented a giant shift in the ontology of nations, now, the technological revolution has caused a nascent revolution in super-power outcomes. What is visible now in the US and the Occident is a process of 'cultural suicide'. The new technological monoliths of the media, and especially social media, have displaced conventional spatial and industrial ontologies. The Industrial Revolution's effects produced win-win turnouts for the nations of the US, Britain, France and Germany – the stalwarts of industrialisation. This meant increased prosperity at home and the ability to 'export' economy and ideology abroad.

Now, what Samuel Huntington calls these 'imagined communities' have become extra-national; media 'globalises' culture, and it means that the effects on their own nation states becomes perilous. This has two reasons. The first is that social media acts like a globalised-spreading ink – vacuous liberal ideas work by watering down the community at home, by weakening the nation state, and spreading like osmosis to communities of like-minded individuals in a virtual world abroad. They build loyalties which are extra-community and therefore dissolve the ties of traditional patterns of community based on real space and time. However, the loyalties they build are not those of the nuanced, gradual real-time shifts of place and time which was witnessed by Medieval Guilds or the Industrial Revolution. Today, these ideas are easily spread through the very nature of 'technological man' – that individuals have morphed into 'Mass Men', as described by the Philosopher Jose Ortega y Gasset. The technological division of labour means that the atomisation of the individual is more pronounced, working in narrower and narrower corners of the cultural web that civilisation has spun. This means that individuals are easily manipulated by the culture of social media extremes, since they have the technical skills of their own work, but not appreciation of wider issues, nor a community of real people to discuss them with. It means that huge and powerful technological elites can export themselves out of their own community and become globalised.

Yet this process leads to the second reason for the current decline of the Occident. Social media does not have the distorting effects in 'mononet' cultures, such as China. Here, by the hegemony of control, social media is driven to conform rather than collapse. Therefore, the process will work to disunite the nation states and communities of the West; the resilience the US showed *vis-a-vis* the old Cold War has vanished. The Chinese, moreover, have a homogenous civilisational nationalist state, based on Han loyalties. This means vicious intolerance to members of its own community – Tibetans and Uighurs. The dialectic outcome of these two competing models of governance – on the one hand autocratic liberal democracy; and on the other, authoritarianism – will be a turning point for humanity. However, the roots of the issues, are not only technological. They go back to the sunrise of the Enlightenment, to values and ontologies which reshaped the world and ushered in the Industrial Revolution. The Enlightenment is dead because its assumptions – the atomised individual, the liberal nation state – have failed to enshrine its security and its community. Once Nietzsche had declared that 'God Is Dead', he envisaged the dark, treacherous seas that humanity would have to sail in a world devoid of spirit, a liberal world view which lacks the moral courage to face death.

China is building a new Silk Road and a high-speed rail link to Europe; Huawei are at the beginning of telecoms revolutions from China outwards, with the fastest cable internet in the world.

It does not take a great leap of imagination to see that the future of wealth and patronage is taking a huge turn eastward. The days of the Occident dictating world ideas are almost over. The Chinese, through soft loans and direct investment, are changing realities in the Caribbean and Africa... everywhere. Brexit was a response – not only to the EU, but to the realignment of strategic thinking; policy has transformed to the axis of the Asia-Pacific region, hence the UK's realignment with the redirection of the US. Europe and the EU are facing retrenchment. The SCO (Shanghai Cooperation Organisation), a military and economic organisation of Russia, China, Tajikistan, Kyrgyzstan, Kazakhstan, and Uzbekistan, is potentially larger now than the EU. Therefore, there will be a reorientation in the power balance to the East, along and through the Silk Roads. The US is recalibrating, moving away from policing the world and attempting to stop the Chinese colossus by protectionism and an anti-Chinese foreign policy. Secession and a split in the Union are not unthinkable, as urban elites continue to alienate the traditionalist periphery. The days of Bretton Woods seem like a distant utopia. However, the new colossus of the Chinese is like reinventing the wheel. It is the next phase of imperialism and capitalism which Lenin predicted, but now with the missionary zeal of technology. It follows the same paradigm as the woes which have been inflicted on post-industrial Europe, along with social dysfunction and poverty and a larger disjoint between rich and poor.

Neo-liberal capitalism is a dangerous addiction we can't shake off. The Asian model of society – predominantly the 'Chinese' model – will add to the environmental problems we now face. There will be an even bigger contraction of democracy and consolidation of power in the oligarchs of the Stans and regimes the Chinese invest in. We are in a period of huge transition. We are mired in pseudo-democratic, irrational structures of government, and blinded by the vernacular of 'growth'. However, we can use a bottom-up approach to realign democracy with the essential meaning of the word: that is, full democracy, not representative democracy. We can opt for real participation, not virtual participation. We can claw back existence from the sense of 'homesickness' we witness in contemporary society. Coronavirus has merely exposed the underlying technical autocracy which is spreading around the world. The attempt to impose technical autocracy through globalisation is in some form of retreat, as the main players in the tech world suffer setbacks *vis-a-vis* the nation states of the periphery. Whilst the elites of the Occidental world, such as Britain and the US, work through accumulative and mason-like institutions such as the WEF, the traditional nations of the world – for example, in the CEE region – force a push-back, i.e. in Poland, Hungary, etc. The most recent attempt at the closing in of the autocratic world has been facilitated by the Coronavirus. It has given the technological and liberal elites a chance to curtail popular sentiment and 'populism'.

The Coronavirus debacle has been represented in the media as a technological problem. The solution to the problem is based on 'modelling'. The UK's response, for example, was based on the modelling of Neil Ferguson's 16 March 2020 paper with Imperial College, London[1]. It predicted the deaths of 500,000 people. This report was based on the method of 'Predictive Modelling' – using the observations of the past to predict the future. Ferguson's alternatives were stated as mitigation or suppression. Therefore, the mitigation policy meant quarantining families, social distancing of the vulnerable – this, it was said, would lead to hundreds of thousands of deaths (stated later as 258,000) over the two years of the simulation. Consequently, the suppression option was preferred, known as 'lockdown'. There are several wild assumptions: the R reproduction rate is assumed at R 2.4, the baseline. It estimates that 81% of the population will acquire the virus and that everyone is equally at risk of catching it. The paper is predicated on the caveat that it all depends on the population's response to lockdown, so there is the initial transference of narrative onto the people. It's down to us. The transmission model used was a hypothetical mathematical one; it assumes all people being equally susceptible to the virus. The occurrence was split one-third in homes, one-third in schools, one-third in the community.

Another assumption was that there would be exponential rises every 6.5 days. It assumed asymptomatic individuals are

50% more infectious than symptomatic ones. However, a lot of factors were left out: ethnicity, age, race, underlying medical conditions, blood groups, genetics (admittedly difficult to ascertain at this stage). This model predicted a 4.4% hospitalisation, 30% critical, and from them a 50% death rate. The model presumes also a near 100% infection rate as it unfolds at the same potency. The numbers, however, do not allow for the fact that many of these people would have died anyway, and as we now know, there has been a blurring of deaths from or with Covid-19. 625,000 people die on average per year in the UK; so, over the span of the two years of the paper, approximately 1.25 million will die.

The paper never received any peer review and was never scrutinised by the government. If they had done so, they would have realised a number of wild assumptions and mistakes. One of the themes mentioned later in the book is the crisis of calibre in the executive, legislative, and administrative fields in the UK. Unlike other autocratic technocracies who employ skilled people in respective fields, the UK employs generalists – often for reasons other than 'expertise'. Ferguson has a background in theoretical physics; he has no formal expertise in modelling, epidemiology, or medicine. This could be excused if it were a one-off oversight by the government. Unfortunately, the UK government has a litany of incompetence in handling crises of any sort. The Foot and Mouth shambles of 2001 led to the killing of 6.5 million animals. This administrative oversight was based on the modelling of Neil Ferguson. There was the BSE in beef scare of 2001, which led to the CJD disease. The Imperial College team had predicted deaths up to approximately 50,000 people. However, a separate study – again at Imperial, led by Neil Ferguson – said his colleagues were 'unjustifiably optimistic'; it was nearer to 136,000. The number of deaths from CJD over the last 30 years is 2826 (National CJD Research and Surveillance Unit University of Edinburgh).

The Bird Flu (H7N9) of 2005 led to the culling of tens of millions of birds. Neil Ferguson was quick to throw his weight behind the ensuing nightmare – his estimate was that 200 million people could die: 'Around 40 million people died in 1918 Spanish

Flu outbreak, there are six times more people on the planet now so you could scale it up to around 200 million people *probably.*' There have been, since 2013, 616 deaths from Bird Flu. Then there was the 2009 Swine Flu, in which Ferguson predicted a 0.4% Case Fatality Rate. That would have been 65,000 UK deaths. There were 457 deaths from Swine Flu up to March 2010 (Independent Review of the UK response to the 2009 influenza pandemic gov.uk). The response to the pandemic was a computer model based on the type commonly used in engineering, for example. These have been proven to be hugely successful extrapolations in the world of physics. However, some systems – for example, predicting stock markets or the weather – do not yield good results, especially when you have so many variables. These ultra-dynamic systems are liable to the vagaries of chaos theory. The code used by the team at Imperial College did not compute seasonality as a variable, when we know the huge influence this has on respiratory problems. The modelled results, as we know, predicted 500,000 deaths. The reality is that in Feb 2021 the numbers are approximately 100,000. That is a 400% error. In Sweden, the only European country not to lock down, a group researching the 'model' tested it to see how the country 'should' have fared. The results illustrated the catastrophic nature of the UK government response based on the modelling. The model said Sweden would have had 96,000 deaths. To date, the country has had 12,500 deaths – a discrepancy of 700%. This is not to trivialise or dehumanise the deaths from Coronavirus, but the lack of efficacy of scientism and government, and the stated response, leaves big holes in the reasons behind the response to the pandemic.

The questions are so big that only a look outside the world of medicine, and further afield in international relations, in globalisation, and in the economic hegemony of capitalism, throws light on the reasons behind the Coronavirus pandemic. But also, the reasons for the response. For the 'response' to crises illuminates the nature of regimes, the zeitgeist behind them, and the systems of culture they are embedded in. Clifford Geertz, the anthropologist, maintained that 'Man is an animal suspended in webs of significance he has himself spun'[2]. The contention of this book is that, in a tiny fraction of time, the webs have been consciously destroyed, piece by piece, in all aspects of life, from the cultural to the economic. This has produced a dangerous physical environment prone to pandemics, a retrenchment of freedom, and technological precarity. Coronavirus, inadvertently, however, offers up a glorious opportunity. From the darkness of Plato's cave, a dim light can be seen. As we shall see with the history of Plagues, they often work that way; whilst the initial effects will be economic retrenchment, a wider revelation may be a reappraisal of the notions of liberal culture and globalisation.

There may also be a realisation of the mendacity of the Chinese. The world will see a movement to populism and nation statism, as witnessed in the growth of former minority parties. This is reflected in the urban-periphery drift witnessed in countries such as the US and the UK. The globalised gulf between the metropolitan elites and traditional communities will foster in an awareness of the vacuity of elitist liberal values. The writing is on the wall for the EU and the idea of the 'Global World'. Brexit, the conservative movements in Poland, Hungary, etc, show a move of feeling away from bureaucratic structures by people dispossessed by neo-liberalism. These countries have rejected the neo-liberal, multi-cultural model. In the days of the Silk Road, trade was seen as a syncretic method of exchange, but not dominance by a small cabal of self-serving multinationals. Decisions today are made in the boardrooms of global companies such as Apple and Google – these organisations exercise huge power but no democracy. The reason Islam and other communal movements are seeing popularity is not hard to decipher. They represent cohesion, community, and a reference point. Western civilisation, based on only a few seconds of post-Enlightenment historical time, chooses the method of exploitation over cooperation, illustrated by world organisations such as the World Bank and the IMF. Global elites have no conscience in the nations they move into – they avoid tax like the plague, and they move profits back out of states and into Western banks. They place money in private schools and other elite organisations, whilst the general poverty of working-class people increases along with debilitating social spheres such as poverty, drugs, deviance, and mental health issues. The new Silk Road is anything but a syncretic exchange of thought or trade. It is the dominance of a small group at the expense of the majority. The dust and toil of the Silk Road has been replaced by the anonymity of the Internet, of unaccountability, of capital accumulation rather than productive industry and manufacturing.

Jared Diamond, in *Guns, Germs and Steel*, echoes the discourse of State evolution to more complex, larger states: 'Over the past 13000 years the predominant trend in human society has been the replacement of smaller, less complex units by larger, more complex ones. Obviously, that is no more than an average long-term trend, with innumerable shifts in either direction.'[3] This paradigm is the essence of an enigma. Notions of progress, development, and growth are coupled with larger, bigger assumptions. This expansion served the purposes of agricultural, then Industrial revolutions. However, the teleology of those systems existed within sustainable communities. Now, the notions of scarcity, fossil fuels, and population crises, mean the teleology is redundant. Larger states and increased global governance have also led to a retraction of freedom and democracy. Elite formation is a natural result of expansive states. Previous historical societies had, in one way or another, the same tendencies, the same issues. By looking at those, we can cast light on the predicaments of modernity, but only if we view life as cyclical and not historical. To view life as historicist is to abnegate responsibility, to systems, to elites, to globalised worlds. Historicism was the failed ideas of an ideal end to structures; the liberal democracy of Hegelian thinking or the Communism of Marx. Only a substantive shift in the paradigm, for both social and environmental reasons, can decouple the modern world away from catastrophe. The end of Enlightenment and the dangers of technological atrophy means a substantive shift in ideological assumptions, a rejection of progress, and a unifying vision that we 'are' the past, that we are thrown into the world, and that there is no inevitability towards a technological solution to modernity.

However, we are now, I sense, at the junction of 'this turn'. By that I mean the nature of the supra-state and globalisation entails we are entering a cyclical turn in world history, signalled by environmental degradation and the decimation of fossil fuels. The State, which had traditional geographical and political limits, has now morphed into a global phenomenon where decisions are made in corporate boardrooms and within global governance. The result is a turning away from this model by the disenfranchised; the urban working-class, the unemployed graduates of American and European cities. Unlike previous revolutions, there is no united front. It is not a predominantly 'working-class' phenomena. It incorporates now a significant population of unemployed, seemingly rootless middle-class youth. As populations struggle for food and water resources, and extraction of minerals becomes critical, states will turn inwards, and liberal dreams will be dashed in the contradictory alliance with neo-liberal capitalism. The liberal democratic ideal is not that 'end of history' revelation which Hegel predicted. The malaise will continue through Chinese-led growth and exploitation of smaller, feeder states. However, it will ultimately lead to a contradiction akin to the Aztec dilemma – the increasing irrationality of human society, of globalisation and the 'forgetting' of the historical teleology of mankind, of competing wars over limited resources.

The Aztecs exploited and enslaved nearby populations to feed exotic chiefdoms of elites, including increasing human sacrifice as a tool for their hegemonic ideology and religion. Eventually, the Aztec kingdom collapsed under these internal strains and from external enemies in the form of the Conquistadors. Whilst the Chinese are the new economic Conquistadors, globalisation ebbs like an historic tide back and forward between hegemonous powers with the horrible spectacle of scarcity looming. The Enlightenment and capitalism disembedded humanity from traditional sustainable material and spiritual structures. The teleology or life purpose of Aristotle was abandoned by the rationalism of the Enlightenment. Therefore, the rejection of Aristotle's view on ethics has left the world at an impasse, especially since the demise of spirit. Aligned to this was the 'atomisation' of the individual, begun in the Enlightenment, and sanctified by capitalism. We are now like Plato's cave-dwellers – chained to the wall of the wasteland by webs of our own making, hoping for the jailers to arrive with the key.

The Plague

In 1849, in the small town of Oran in Algeria, following the French colonisation of the country, a cholera epidemic broke out which devastated the local population. It was first noticed that rats were dying – flushed up from rivers, crawling helpless through the streets, squealing from hunger. The local Prefect of the district, along with colleagues on the council, were told of the problem but did nothing. An errant doctor noticed that his colleague was becoming ill, and informed the authorities. They would not entertain the notion that anything serious was happening and warned the doctor to abstain from scare-mongering. The doctor's colleague died. Then a few more died, but the council declared there was nothing wrong and, besides, business and trade was the priority. They were building a new coffee plantation and the French were irritated by the council's inactivity. Production must go on.

The council assured the people there were the correct contingency plans in place. The government was ready for such things. A brass band played 'La Marseillaise' in an empty town square, and the populace clapped. But the hospitals were filling up with people, then bodies. There were no more beds in the hospital, and the locals were carrying corpses to the tomb carts which passed by in the dark like sulking tea clippers to collect the dead. The council introduced quarantine, but the people, who lived on a largely agrarian smallholder diet, were unable to turn over the earth, to till the soil. Soon there was no food in the town and no deliveries were allowed in.

The only business was death and viruses. It seeped through rivers and crawled into the little yellow-coloured houses which sat above the town staring. It crawled into the water barrels. The town was quarantined; there was no news in or out. The only beneficiaries were the French Catholic priests preaching the vengeance of God, and a smuggler from Algiers who left bread and fruit at the village mosque, for exorbitant prices, at night, under cover of the dark skies. There were a few citizens who tried to escape the town, to run into the hills – but they were shot dead by the Police. Looting began, and there were more shootings.

The people, like the Pitcairn Islanders before them, resorted to cannibalism. Paper money became worthless; even the smuggler wouldn't accept the dirty bubonic notes. A Jewish man in the market was beaten to death. A group of locals formed a militia; they had suffered for years, they wanted justice, reparations, and any resistance was against them. It is the apogee of humanity and despair – all the grubby, greedy traits come squirming out; the ones that had been hidden under the veneer of normalcy.

This, essentially, was the plot of Albert Camus's novel *The Plague* (*La Peste*), written in 1947. It reverberates now in the light of the Ebola and now the Coronavirus spectres. Those modes of human isolation and desperation, which, although seeming catastrophic, can have a joyous epiphany, but only if we recognise the absurdity of the neo-liberal paradigm. For the 'Plague' is just a euphemism for a plague of materialism, a wasteland of consumerism, of dysfunctional culture. The Plague in Oran is a tempest forewarning of a new pestilence; a pestilence which brings dysfunctional societies, and places profit above health. The Plague is born in the shape of technology, in machines, in the alienation of man in the computer age, in the destruction of community, the collapse of family and spirituality, and the end of real happiness. It is not the fate of the dead which is the only horror; the horror is how the Plague affects the living. The worry is that the habit of isolation, of despair, of the eclipse of liberty, becomes the norm and only memories of the past remain.

Coronavirus highlights the absurdity of life; the tenuous link to mortality, and the futile nature of contemporary notions of 'progress'. The protagonist Rieux speaks of not heroism, or 'key' people, but 'common decency' to be shown by all. The Coronavirus has illustrated the banality of us all; there are no heroes, merely millions of decent, unremarkable people – the factory workers, nurses, street cleaners. These people are the vigilant, the clean, who can see the aspects of the Plague in the echelons, in the leaders.

Alexis De Tocqueville, the great observer of democracy, wrote in 1858 that *'un virus d'une espece nouvelle et inconnue'* ('a virus of new and unknown species') was virulent. The new virus that De Tocqueville was describing was not a natural virus, but that of the French Revolution. De Tocqueville was one of those rare commentators, like Edmund Burke or Kurt Vonnegut, who could encapsulate epochs in a sentence. The new virus today is the wedding of technology and liberal sentiments. There is now a passage to a technological phase of society, combined with an authoritarian end of democracy – an ability to suppress dissent whilst delivering the minimum soporific of tolerance for homo sapiens. The new virus, the 'Technological Turn', entails a technical explanation of life. Everything within modernity – from computers, to knowledge, to leisure – is determined by offering technical solutions. Scientific models, such as the 'Imperial' modelling response to Coronavirus, abdicate responsibility away from government to 'rationality', or machines. Human beings can accept this, as the world increasingly appears as a technological playing field. Human agency is less and less, from the diagnosis at the car mechanic, to the NHS consultant, to algorithms of social media opinion forming, a removal of 'participatory' models of citizenship. Human beings have less and less communication with reality.

The model is extended eastwards through globalisation and development to ensure the participation in the new brave stage of technocratic authoritarianism. Technology, through the media, and behaviourism, allows this to be dressed up in a familiar attire of 'liberal democracy'. The new stage is sold as progress, development. However, the move through technology is only the continuation of a process of disembedding of humankind from history. It began precisely with the sacralisation of the State, and then the rationalisation of humans into productive and industrial societies. Man was removed from history and planted in the factory, bureaucracy, and now, in a periphery mode, as part of the technological world. This was worked out in a post-Enlightenment social contract whereby humankind is given by the State titular privileges (health insurance and 'rights') in exchange for a Panopticon of servitude. The realms of private belief – whether that be religion, civil society groups, or chat in the agricultural cooperative – were, historically, intimate. The development of medias has meant the move of beliefs away from a private sphere into a public sphere. Therefore, if you can dominate these fields, you dominate a large swathe of humankind. In the realms of social media, there is the further extension whereby proffered beliefs need to accord with the opinion-forming elites, although people are given the illusion of participation. What is really happening on social media and the internet is the framing of opinion, ideas, to the uniform.

De Tocqueville saw the threat of 'democracy' and 'equality', in the sense that they require a 'general will' to be effective. This general will has been ably constituted by the new technology and media. Therefore, the transference from liberty to equality modes is a chimera. Liberty was a real construction, one which was akin to John Stuart Mill's ideas about lack of constraints. Here, equality is seen as a threat to liberty, as equality is represented in a type of majority opinion, the triumph of 'public' belief. A read of John Stuart Mill's *On Liberty* (1859) is a quick antidote for anyone who believes in progress in its contemporary meaning.

De Tocqueville felt the pushing out of equality modes meant the eclipsing of liberty, for the fear of non-conforming becomes arbitrary, the individual increasingly conforms to the norms of titular equality. The 'technological turn', moreover, has shown that liberalism has been bypassed in modernity elsewhere – from China, Russia, to Turkey. Liberalism was not needed as a stage to modernism. These nations, and increasingly large parts of the world, are going all-in on technocratic authoritarianism. The Coronavirus response has shown that they were largely correct. In China, for example, the fast-tracking to GDP, consumer culture, has shown that the Western phase for 'titular' access to what liberals call 'rights', 'equality', etc, were merely a smokescreen for the reality above; the incorporation of humankind in rational productive relations. The titanic error of liberal philosophers from the Enlightenment onwards, from Locke to Rawls, was to deny spirit, to deny that belief mattered. By this, we don't mean 'religious' belief *per se*, but the conviction they held was that the rationalised world really was 'the end of history'.

The new virus of technological liberalism is a development of societal relations rooted in the technical development of society. For the majority of the existence of homo sapiens on this planet (approximately the last 200,000 years), food consumption involved varieties of hunting and gathering. In fact, in hindsight, we would have to argue that hunting and gathering was the only really sustainable method. Different bands of humans developed agriculture at varying rates (some did not, i.e. the Australian Aborigines). The origins of this variation, however, has nothing to do with intelligence. Franz Boas, the anthropologist, showed how human brains are essentially similar across continents. There is, therefore, the dilemma of explaining the different stages of agricultural development which led to the dominance of some groups. The reason behind the varied trend is one of geographical location. This was allied to the fact that some groups, such as Eurasians, were able to ally agriculture with the domestication of animal species which were unavailable elsewhere. Farming made sense; it meant you could grow an exponentially larger crop than you would obtain by hunting and gathering. However, the acceleration of agriculture occurred with the use of animals, such as cows, yaks, sheep, and chickens. These animals not only provided superior levels of protein, but also added a cyclical benefit of manure and agricultural 'equipment' to plough fields, etc. Increased agriculture developed into agricultural surplus, which meant expanding populations. The ability to store food was another advantage over hunting and gathering. It meant there were excess stocks, which became useful for a growing number of specialists within these communities who had adopted the sedentary lifestyle associated with farming. It was the development of organised structures of governance, into chiefdoms and kingships, which created a stratification of society whereby some would rule and administer, and others could be soldiers, farmers, etc.

Eurasians were also able to domesticate horses and donkeys, which gave them a means of transport and a formidable weapon in times of conflict with neighbours (usually conflict over arable land and resources). This explains the relative ease at which Cortez and Pizarro were able to subdue the Aztecs and Incas. Eurasia had gifted some humans with a paradisiacal environment of good soils, abundant edible crops, and domesticable animals. However, there was one catch. That was the transfer of germs and viruses from animal livestock to humans, which had not happened in hunter gatherer communities. Living in proximity to animals came with a Janus-faced smile; the same smirk which sees the Chinese economic miracle today proliferating the world with animal-borne viruses. The technological 'progress' of mankind, exacerbated by neo-liberal modes of economy and culture- means the virulent acceleration of existential threats.

One of the main issues facing the world today is a misreading of history or, more disturbing, a deliberate betrayal of historical narrative. It is that the vast majority of killer diseases have been born from interaction with animals; this is self-evident in that smallpox, plague, etc, are a direct result of close affinity to livestock. Not only Bill Gates, but some of the world's leading scientists have warned of possible pandemics which could wipe out the world's population. Viruses can destroy 99% of a population. Rationalism in science approaches the problem with a salvo of vaccines and cures for AIDS, Cholera, Ebola, and the recent discovery of a vaccine for Coronavirus. It is seen as a 'technological' or a 'medical' problem – the vast corpus of scientific reductionist thinking which reduces things to its constituent parts, rather than dealing with the real issues. The contention of this book is that, whilst vaccines, of course, are beneficial to human populations, we need to look at the wider issue, a holistic analysis of a recurring historical problem. Within the laws of thermodynamics there is the idea that if you don't treat the source of the scourge, these catastrophes will continue with increased entropy. Unless the world faces the contradictions evident in the neo-liberal globalisation project – from viruses to the environment, and also the existential threats of nuclear war and global warming – then we will most likely face extinction as a species.

Plagues change the future course of history; that is evident in the Justinian Plague which decimated the Byzantine and Sassanid Empires, to the epidemics brought by Europeans to the Americas post-Columbus. The Black Death caused epochal biblical changes to mid-14th Century Europe and the late medieval period. The Bubonic Plague is endemic within rodent populations, and it sometimes migrates through zoonotic transfer to humans. The origins of the Bubonic Plague are not clear, although recent research suggests either the Tibetan plateau in Western China or the Tien Shan mountain area of the Chinese-Kyrgyz border. It was the interactions and conduit of the road of the caravanserais which enabled the efficient globalisation of the Plague. State formation and expansion, through the Mongols, in the 13th Century meant that the vast Eurasian landmass became part of a unified Mongol Empire. There then was a kind of microbial unification of the world. By the mid-1340s, the Plague had been delivered to the Mongol khanate (region) of the Golden Horde, and moved to the Russian lands. The Mongol ruler, Khan Jani Beg, then brought the Plague to the Crimea in the siege of Kaffa. The Genoese merchants of Kaffa then fled via Constantinople, thereby bringing the virus into Europe, the Middle East, and North Africa, killing at least one-third of the population.

There are seminal similarities in the social implications then as now. However, Plague 'uncovers' essential attributes of systems; inequalities, unfettered development, environmental decay. Boccaccio notes in the *Decameron* (1353) that traditional societal bonds began to dissolve: parents abandoning children, brothers leaving brothers, in fear of the Plague. The Plague led to xenophobia and attacks on neighbours. The Plague resulted in workers and agricultural workers abandoning their jobs from fear of contamination. There are clear cyclical repetitions in the world of the Plague, just as now we have isolation, furloughs, and the hoarding of vaccines. However, most importantly, the Plague hastened the demise of existing orders, such as the feudal one. It was the death knell of feudalism, already weakened by a myriad of afflictions. Famine, debt, agricultural crises, and the end of the 'Pax Mongolica' (the end of the East-West trade routes) had, in the previous century, severely weakened the world of medieval Europe. The Black Death meant a halving of the population but also provided an economic stimulus in rising wealth of the populations, due to a bloat of goods, animals, etc. This led to a period of wage inflation and then, as in our own Keynesian boom-bust cycles, to inflation. The nobility of Europe had a vested interest in warfare in eliciting lost incomes; hence the Hundred Years War's longevity. The nobility also squeezed the peasantry in a series of tax increases, leading to numerous peasant rebellions around Europe. Consequently, the Plague had the effect of starting a nascent political sensibility across Europe, as well as fomenting semblances of agrarian capitalism. In Byzantium, the Plague signalled its collapse and the arrival of the Ottomans.

Therefore, Plagues have the capacity to hasten the demise of already weak and unstable countries. Plagues magnify and accelerate existing endemic traits. The massive impact on the US and Europe of Covid will have civilisational consequences for these countries which exhibit weak and irrational government; it is no surprise that the relative 'success' of Asian nations has been achieved through a homogeneity of culture unseen in the West. But this would be to misunderstand the reasons *behind* the Coronavirus shock and its causes. We should be more focussed on the wider reasons *why* Coronavirus happened, rather than on how effective authoritarian states are at dealing with pandemics. If we address the former, then there is no need for the latter. If there can be any benefit to the catastrophe of Coronavirus, it is what the future may bring; a dialectic which, although deathly, may signal a new realignment of people against materialism and a return to pre-Enlightenment notions of the primacy of family, community, and the environment.

Apocalypse Now:
The Evolution of Viruses

Large surpluses and the use of livestock led to increasing and denser populations. The most dangerous germs in history have been evolved from livestock, whether that be Aids, Smallpox, Measles, or TB. Although there had been a historical transmission of trade along the Silk Road routes, it was only with Columbus and the opening of the Americas that continents, which had previously been geographically isolated, began to open up. The Conquistadores' arrival into the empire of the Aztecs was more than symbolic, because it illustrated the catastrophic impact viruses can have. Viruses are not wilful or bad – they have just evolved, like other organisms, in an attempt to be more efficient. The better the microbes at spreading disease then the more they are selected in 'Natural Selection' and so on. Viruses use various methods for transferring themselves from animal to animal, person to person. For example, Salmonella is passed on through the victim eating infected eggs or meat. Anisakiasis is passed on through eating raw fish, as in sushi. The AIDS virus originated from eating wild African monkeys. Some viruses use mosquitoes, tsetse flies, etc, to transmit their ills to another animal, as in Malaria. The Bubonic Plague was passed on through fleas which moved from rat to rat. Viruses such as Flu, Whooping Cough, and the common cold, use coughing and sneezing as a way to transmit the microbes. Cholera uses diarrhoea to expunge the microbes into rivers, toilets, etc, in unclean environments, to spread the virus.

In an attempt to get rid of viruses, the body uses a variety of methods to stem the assault on the body. When we have a fever, it is the attempt to defeat the microbes through heat. When the immune system gets into action, it allows white cells to infiltrate and kill the microbes. Therefore, the body develops antibodies which, in the future, are used as a defence mechanism against further bouts of the disease. However, lots of viruses are able to mutate, such as the flu virus, and come back to haunt us. Aids and Malaria are skilled in coming back with another form, another mutation. However, natural selection is probably the greatest natural resistor to this trend, but the problem with natural selection is it can take thousands of years. Why was it that when the Conquistadores landed in Villa Rica, with a force of 500 soldiers, they were able to decimate a warrior-like force of millions of Aztecs? When Cortez arrived, and subsequent landings of Conquistadores, the local Aztecs noticed a strange thing. Whilst their own people were dropping like the proverbial flies, the Spanish seemed immune. The Conquistadores appeared on white horses and seemed invincible to the diseases, such as Smallpox, which the Europeans exported. This was because the Europeans had been exposed to these pathogens over thousands of years, thus, through natural selection, making them immune. Through natural selection, the ill die out and those communities are less likely to pass on the virus. This explains how the Europeans colonised the Americas and brought disease, and why Europeans trying to colonise Africa suffered heavily in the eighteenth and nineteenth centuries.

What is unique among modern epidemics is the rapidity of transmission. When humans existed as bands of hunter gatherers and not living in close proximity with animals, it made epidemics unlikely. The Bubonic Plague, which killed one-quarter of the European population between 1346 and 1352, was a result of the changing social landscape of Europe. It was a period of population growth in urban centres and the concentration of animals and livestock in confined, unhygienic conditions. Although we may consider ourselves to have progressed since the Middle Ages, the conditions in which we keep animals, especially in Asia, has not changed. The increasing frequency of proximity of populations is the main cause of modern problems such as Coronavirus. The Influenza virus killed 20 million people in the years after the First World War. The problem with Influenza is that it can mutate into different versions. Therefore, the type of epidemics which spread quickly, killing large percentages of populations, are called 'crowd diseases' – the likes of Measles and Coronavirus.

Coronavirus needs new populations to spread in; hence the fact that when people are isolated, cases decline and eventually the disease wears off, having killed a certain percentage and given antibodies to those survivors who were infected. Small indigenous tribes do get viruses – such as Leprosy and Yellow Fever, for example – but they are not 'crowd diseases'. The relevance of crowd diseases is for large urban populations where there is an influx of livestock. Therefore, we can argue that epidemics and pandemics are exclusive to what we call 'civilisation'. Without civilisation, there would be no Coronavirus. The Black Death arrived in 1346 courtesy of the new Silk Road and Chinamen trading furs which contained fleas infested with Bubonic Plague. The new reality is that the Silk Road has morphed into a globalised world where pathogens, from one population to another, can be carried in the time it takes to fly from Peking to LA. You don't have to be a red-flag-waving Marxist to see the dangers of globalisation. Therefore agriculture, then cities, started our long relationship with 'crowd diseases'. Probably the first cataclysmic impact was on the Romans, when Plague hit between AD 165/180. This plague killed millions of people and arrived in Rome courtesy of the new international trade routes of the Roman Empire. Likewise, the Bubonic Plague which struck Europe in 1346 was a result of the opening up of a trade route in the East: The Silk Road. Now, the problems of antiquity, which we thought were one-offs and couldn't happen again, have come back to haunt us in the form of the Coronavirus. This is also due to something called the 'availability heuristic' which we touch on later. The origins of viruses of Influenza, Smallpox, and Measles, are all descended from animals and our close proximity to animals, particularly cows, sheep, pigs, and ducks. Whilst 'modern' diseases, such as leptospirosis from dogs and brucellosis from cows, are only transferred from animal to human, the older killers have evolved over thousands of years to be able to transfer from an animal-to-human system to a human-to-human system. Not all of these diseases are bad, but some are deadly. With some of the human-to-human diseases, their effects are short-lived and people recover; for example, the fever which hit East Africa in 1959 and infected millions was short-lived, and most recovered. Some viruses are so lethal that they kill everyone that come into contact. For example, the 'Laughing Sickness', 'Kuru', was passed on through cannibalism. A rather unfortunate name for the victim who, having devoured his friend/enemy/mother-in-law, then suffered a slow, fatal death. The Last Supper, you could say. The 'English Sweating Sickness', which paralysed Europe with fear for fifty years after 1485, had nothing to do with the English and their penchant for sitting out in the midday sun. It killed William Compton and was extremely rapid; once struck, it caused constant sweating and could kill in hours. In contrast, other viruses which jumped from animals to humans have remained around, for example, Lyme Disease, Lassa Fever, and AIDS.

It was the arrival of Cortez and Pizarro which spread the likes of smallpox into the Americas. But that begs the question: why did it not work the other way around? Why did the native Indians in the Americas not pass on their germs to the Conquistadores? In fact, this point is doubly important, as it impinges upon the central argument of this book. We already know that 'crowd diseases' were eminent amongst large urban populations. For many years that has been the accepted narrative of transmission, which is correct. Tenochitlan and other cities in the New World were of a similar range population-wise as cities in Eurasia. So, why did the Americas not evolve their own set of viruses like in Eurasia? There are a few reasons for this. Firstly, there wasn't a well-trodden route of trade, as in the paths during the Roman Empire and the routes out of China westwards. South, Central, and North America did not have a passage of trade similar to the ones which linked Europe, Asia, and Africa. Consequently, if an outbreak of disease occurred, it tended to be localised. There is no evidence of major outbreaks in the Americas in the days of the Old World/New World axis. The other reason is the 'type' of livestock which the respective worlds domesticated. In the Americas, the Ice Age, which ended approximately 100,000 years ago, destroyed about 90% of large land mammals. However, in

Eurasia there was no impact on the likes of cows and pigs. Therefore, the evolution of microbes was able to work due to the close alliance of men and large domesticated animals. In the Americas, some animals were domesticated, i.e. turkey, guinea, and dogs, but were not huge herding-type beasts, hence this reduced the likelihood of crowd-type diseases.

The contention of many scientists now is that 'zoonotic transfer' between animals and humans is becoming more common; that human 'development', i.e. economic development, has a hidden cost in the cost-benefit ratios of neo-liberal capitalism. There is no such thing as a free lunch. The domestication of animals and the increasing proximity of trade come at a huge and dangerous cost to homo sapiens. The Coronavirus, emanating from China, is perhaps the most disturbing. It is disturbing for other reasons than the obvious – the death of millions of people. But we are familiar with this type of devastating virus, whether it be Ebola, Aids, etc. What is frightening about the Coronavirus is the fact that these viruses are on the increase and, if we do not change fundamental animal-human relationships, they will get worse. For most of human history, the essential problems of existence have been linked to a failure of moral teleology, a forgetting of the essence of humanity, and a pursuit by elites of narrow, destructive interests from industrialisation to globalisation, the destruction of habitat, and the irrational belief in 'progress'.

Animal Farm: China and 'Zoonotic Transfer'

What was described above is the standard model of the history of viruses like Bubonic Plague, Aids, Coronavirus, and their transmission. They have prospered, as we have seen, in dense population areas and with the evolution of agriculture and urban populations. However, one of the most worrying developments is the occurrence of these killer viruses in isolated, indigenous areas. What causes the outbreak of more and more viruses in rural areas? David Quammen in *Spillover: Animal Infections and the Next Pandemic,* writes:

'We cut the trees; we kill the animals or cage them and send them to markets. We disrupt ecosystems, and we shake viruses loose from their natural hosts. When that happens, they need a new host. Often, we are it.'[1]

The majority of new dangerous diseases infecting humans are transmitted from animal to human. However, it overlooks a wider root cause, which places the cause of pandemics of the crowd disease-type firmly as a by-product of global trade. New viruses are increasing and, worst of all, the number of viruses moving from animals to humans is increasing. It is estimated that as many as 75% of new diseases are linked to animals. The MERS virus was transferred from camels to humans. Coronavirus is thought to have originated in bats. The Coronavirus is nothing new in terms of dangerous viruses. What is new is that the number of these epidemics is increasing and, it seems, the viruses are becoming deadlier. For example, the SARS virus which originated in China caused the deaths of 700 people and managed to get into over 30 countries. Some viruses such as Zika are able to mutate and establish themselves from continent to continent. With the increase in human populations, especially urban centres, and the massive increase in deforestation, logging, destruction of habitat, we are bringing animals too close to humans. Some cultures, most notably in China, have cultural practices which exacerbate these problems, by caging and living in close proximity to wild animals. The bad news is that there are a large number of pathogens out there which are yet to be found. Some viruses are not so easily dispersed, such as Ebola; but others, like Coronavirus, are easily spread. The proximity of human to animal habitats is clearly visible in the pandemic of Lyme Disease which is afflicting many parts of the world, particularly in the US. New housing and urban populations put humans right next to forested areas where, before, there was no interaction between humans and animals. Now cats and dogs bring the ticks into the houses of humans.

The problem is not only one of proximity, but also the nature of scientific method. Ever since the Enlightenment, science has been driven by the scientific reductionist method; thereby, things are broken down into constituent parts and a solution/cure is attempted. However, the world is like a human body – you cannot treat merely one aspect or one organ without examining its impact on other parts. Later in the book, I use the analogy of the *Anna Karenina* principle to suggest that we need a holistic, encompassing treatment of problems. A happy family can only exist if the constituent parts of the family do things correctly. Coronavirus and pathogens are symptomatic of a wider malaise – the globalisation of production, and the problem of overpopulation. For this reason, scientists such as Richard Ostfeld, a scientist at the Cary Institute of Ecosystem Studies in New York, have developed the idea of 'planetary health'. Without human stress on the environment there would be no environmental degradation or climate change, and there would be no mass pandemics. It is the encroachment of homo sapiens into the natural world which is the cause of our present crisis. In built-up urban areas there is a proliferation of the so-called 'wet markets', like the one in Wuhan, thought to be the source of Coronavirus. The market in Wuhan, however – despite the denials of the Chinese – was also selling a menagerie of wild animals unused to close proximity with humans. The market, which also contained snack bars and restaurants, was home to caged wolf pups, turtles, scorpions, crocodiles, foxes, and squirrels. The same spectacle can be found in other Asian markets, and also in Africa. In Africa, you can find monkeys, birds, and other animals for sale next to garbage and waste water.

The wet markets provide an ideal breeding ground for what scientists call the 'spill over effect'; it means the transference of pathogens from one species to another. In the natural habitat of these animals this would not happen, as they would not inhabit such a confined space. Before globalisation and before the movement of people to urban centres, there were less people dependent on animal trading to earn a living; now the lights of the city attract people from the countryside. It all boils down to the type of socio-economic system we have in place. It is no good advertising Coca-Cola unless you have a client base, and that client base will do anything to be part of the dream. That is the moral ideological assumptions built into advertising and culture.

Also, the economic paradigm is set in place by the World Bank and the IMF – and global capital is the main feature of 'development'. The export of wood and resources from the periphery countries to the 'Occident' means devastated landscapes and habitats; it means the pushing together of species at the periphery. Huge increases in populations squeeze habitats of other species. All of the above would point to the bush markets of Asia and Africa as being the source of the problem. If we close down these markets, then the problem will go away. Unfortunately, just as many of us go to Tesco for our food, millions of people go to bush markets. The core of the problem is an unpalatable one for most Western tastes – the problem isn't 'them'; it is 'us'. The reason for inflated, packed bush markets on the fringes of Lagos and Wuhan is a response to global neo-liberal capitalism – people moving from traditional sustainable livelihoods into the metropolis for the promise of work, for the promise of the lifestyle which we value so highly in the west. The reason for the exodus to the city is the concerted effort of 'development' agencies and the referees of neo-liberal greed: The World Bank, the IMF. The reason for these horrors is the concentration of power and wealth amongst the elites of the world, and their demand for more and more profit and dividends. Often organisations from the Occident highlight 'micro' reasons for problems, rather than looking at the 'macro' situation; they are often full of the soundbites of the West – the view from the Occident. For example, in its list of Sustainable Development Goals, the UN says:

'Make cities and human settlements inclusive, safe, resilient and sustainable.'[2]

These soundbites such as 'inclusive' and 'sustainable' are meaningless for the vast majority of the new urban poor. The UN Sustainable Development Goals talk of 'economic growth ' and 'industrialisation'. It is like when Franz Boas, the anthropologist, spoke of *Kulturbrille* or 'Culture Glasses' – the endemic failing of elites in the West that see problems through their own paradigm; the very paradigm which is on the brink of causing catastrophic climate and health problems.

Since the mid-twentieth century, the population of urban areas has increased dramatically. For example, in 1950 the urban population was 30%; in 2018 it was 55% and rising. The majority of these increases (90%) happen in Asia and Africa. There is now an increasing demand for processed foods, industrialised meat production and dairy products – the same items we in the West buy at Tesco. There has been what can only be called a livestock revolution; from 1980 to 2020 there has been a 200% increase in meat production in Asia and Africa. This extrapolated to 2050 would mean an increase of calories intake from 200 to 400 calories per day for livestock products![3]. What the UN calls 'sustainable' was already in place; in fact, it had evolved with nature for the last 10,000 years when Africans and Asians began domesticating animals. What is unsustainable is the new era of neo-liberal economic growth. The urbanisation of areas has led to associated problems, such as air and water pollution, a lack of healthcare facilities, and a rise also in the non-transmitted diseases such as cancer, blood pressure, etc. These new demands lead to the encroachment on wilderness areas and increase the likelihood of zoonotic disease. These zoonotic diseases are transmitted through meat and dairy products and other animal products. The WHO estimates that 61 per cent of all human diseases now are zoonotic in nature, and this statistic is increasing.

Therefore, the predominant driver of zoonotic disease is the change in land use and agricultural practice for countries in Asia and Africa, as well as the migration trend into cities. Unregulated encroachment on rural land develops without adequate planning. For example, building on previous flood plains can lead to extensive waterlogging in the environment, which can lead to water born infectious disease. For example, moving into rural habitats in Cambodia, Thailand, India, Bangladesh, and Madagascar, led to the infamous 'Nipah' virus. This was due to the proximity of fruit bats to humans and livestock, and transmitting zoonotic disease. McFarlane et al[4] showed that 22% of infectious diseases are linked to land use and land cover change. Organisations such as the UN and their scientific envoys employ the 'reductionist' method of simplifying and demarcating zoonotic disease into easy narratives: dirty markets, poor health services, shanty towns and slums. These, however, are merely expressions of underlying formative effects from political and economic drivers. Cradock and Hinchliffe maintain: 'Who gets sick and where, are not simply ecological or demographic outcomes. Often forces of a political and economic nature create disease, and more crucially, determine the manner of its management and control. Development interventions can displace people to marginal places, making them vulnerable to disease.'[5]

Hence the narrative focusses on the consequences rather than the macro or causal reasons behind zoonotic transfer. The number of new pathogens is on the increase. In a report in 2004, in a sample of water from the Sargasso Sea there was identified an incredible 1.2 million new genes, 1800 species, and 148 new bacterial phylotypes, which illustrated that the microbial diversity is increasing or is considerably higher than previously thought. These microbes can move from species to species, recombine, and create new pathogens. This, together with fertile conditions for zoonotic transfer, is a potential health disaster of epic proportions – the type we see now with Coronavirus.

However, the primary driver of disease is the political-economic framework. This has many reasons: the individual political schema of a particular regime, the global economic system, and the now increased alignment of global capital with organisations such as the WHO. The Ebola disease which struck the area of Liberia-Sierra Leone and Guinea region was largely a result of socio-economic pressures on marginalised people in poverty. The reality of the post-colonial existence for these areas is clearly evident. The post-colonial era established complicit government in these areas, who played the neo-liberal game and were therefore rewarded with 'development' money from the likes of the World Bank. This money was used to propagate an elitist system imitative of the Occident. The elites dominate resources and do not invest in health systems or address living conditions, sanitation, or basic services. This, in turn, has led to an epidemic of warfare (there have been over 100 conflicts in Africa between 1989 and 2000), causing the displacement of over 40 million people on a huge scale, often moving to slums in urban environments and succumbing to Ebola and other diseases. The solution is not knocking down slums or shanty towns, or cleaning up markets in Wuhan Province. Unfortunately, the problem is much bigger than that. It is so big that it needs a paradigm shift away from economic and political systems in both the Occident and the Orient.

Will Modern Society Collapse?

There is nothing new about civilisations or empires collapsing. Those dystopian futures, much the subject of literature and film – from Ursula Le Guin's *City of Illusions* to *A Canticle for Leibowitz* by Walter M. Miller – are based on what has gone before, and they are not only likely, but inevitable. In *A Canticle for Liebowitz*, the Albertian monks – holed out in the ruins of a deserted monastery – piece together the remnants of civilisation following a nuclear war. It stresses the cyclical nature of societies. It sees the battle to form states in hostile environments, then expansion of material progress, and then the withering away of the telos that underwrote the initial success. The reason the Coronavirus shock appears so frightening is that we have lived through a period of (relative) European peace. World War 2 was the last war which impacted Europe; however, the glue of bonds which kept European society together is disintegrating. Collapses, moreover, do not take on the appearance of a singularity – that is, one underlying factor or cause. What historians are increasingly recognising is that societies collapse precisely due to complexity.

One of the most intriguing collapses was the downfall of the Bronze Age civilisations in 1177 BC. Traditional accounts of the collapse of the Bronze Age world system across the Mediterranean and Anatolian regions portray the collapse due to a raiding group of mysterious 'Sea Peoples' who pillaged and rampaged coastal regions of Ancient Egypt, etc. This collapse is especially interesting because it was the progenitor of globalisation; the first global world system based on trade. There were extensive trading circles in the region – from Minoan Crete to Egypt, to the Hittite Kingdom in Anatolia, and to the Mycenaeans. Between 1400 and 1200 BC saw the rise of the Assyrians as a great power. When the anthropologist Malinowski posited his idea of the 'Kula Ring' – a trading circuit based on shells – around the periphery of Papua

New Guinea, he had outlined a type of 'world system'. This was essentially a trading conduit between various peoples, with the currency being shells. Traders risked their lives to trade shells and bracelets around separated islands. The Egyptians during the Bronze Age period used Nubian Gold as a type of currency to attract traders. Amongst this were the usual battles and assertions for trade routes and power. As Hittites and Egyptians fought a battle at Qadesh in 1274, the Myceans were underwriting revolt in Hittite Anatolia. The vassal state of Ugarit was destroyed in 1190 BC, along with abandoned or destroyed Hittite sites throughout Anatolia. Mainland Greece suffered massive destruction, all around this time. Historians have elaborated on famine, earthquakes, the invasions of those 'Sea Peoples', and climate change (drier region). However, the evidence suggests that the decline in populations was not tantamount to a particular explanation. The sudden collapse of civilisations, without adequate explanation, has figured in histories of sudden entropy of the Mayans, the Indus Valley Civilisation (Harappa). What was noted by Colin Renfrew in his seminal *Systems Collapse as Social Transformation*, was that there are prominent features of a systems collapse. The collapse of a centralising administrative organisation, the eclipse of an elite class, the break-up of a centralised economy, and possible population contraction. However, for my analysis, the prominent feature is the adoption by these societies of some type of 'currency' within an expanded economic system. In the Bronze Age cultures, this could have been gold, bronze or copper, but the defining feature is a form of *globalisation*. At the heart of the problem is the adoption of inter-trade; all systems initially benefit from what economists call 'comparative advantage', thereby one state produces for example silk, the other produces metals. The system works whilst terms of trade work equally and each state benefits in the 'Kula Ring'. However, elites seek to increase their cut, and embark on military or cultural means to assimilate other regions (due to raw materials, oil, etc). Therefore, the system becomes destabilised, ostensibly due to the greed of elites, patronage, and tribute, etc.

Globalised systems, by their nature, suffer from the seeds of their own destruction. Often societies 'forget' the objectives or culture which made them successful, the teleology of tradition. This was clear with the Easter Islanders, who, for unknown reasons, suddenly embarked on a spiritual building of statues and deforestation which led to ecocide. Although the epochal change 'appears' to be economic, it is, however, mostly ideological (although not exclusively). That is, the elites embark on a schema for ideological reasons. Often elites develop ideological adjustments – for example, the 'institutionalisation' of monotheistic religions; the obsessive racial theories of Nazi Germany; the diffusion of 'Identity Politics' in the contemporary era. If the ideology is based on authentic thought, it can be positive and defining. However, ideologies which attack the traditional teleology can be divisive and destructive to society. Once global or cyclical issues arise, there is a penchant for societies to find scapegoats for their woes. The Aztecs embarked on increasingly debilitating sacrificial systems which weakened their previous authority and separated them from the 'commoners'. The Tsars resorted to 'pogroms' against Jews to assert popularity. In the UK and US, 'nativism' – or the perceived failure of the white indigenous population to recognise 'racism' within their culture – is used as a means by the Brahmin left to 'blame' the working-class for what are other structural problems. Identity politics is used to divide and rule, and obfuscate real reform. The current movement away from consensus to periphery issues has caused a division within elites, but most notable, the alienation of indigenous communities. When the UK moved from a manufacturing country to a service economy in the 1980s, they had changed the ontology of the regime. From being one based on production and labour, it moved to one based on capital accumulation through speculative banking and financial market accumulation. Therefore, they had removed the ideological bedrock that was the Industrial Revolution. The problem with these types of 'service/financial' economies is that they are highly susceptible to financial shock or confidence; hence, the run to gold during financial implosions.

Likewise, what is now termed 'globalisation' is a world system based on global trade and capital flows, but ultimately diminishing the individual nation states and increasing the exploitation of labour. Eventually, these members recognise the unfairness in the globalised system and adopt nativist, populist policies. A 'Kula Ring' inevitably produces winners and losers, trade deficits and trade surpluses, and states, such as the US and China, needing to redress the balance. The ring is weakened by some states exerting military influence, i.e. the US, China, in the new hierarchy. Through these disturbances, the institutions of world governance (The UN, World Bank, the EU) lose legitimacy and appear weak (the 'League of Nations' syndrome). There will be a competition in fiat currency – Dollars or Chinese Renminbi. Again, the fundamental *raison d'etre* of formation of a global system works whilst the 'commoners' feel part of the system. However, once elites dominate the system for personal benefit, the weaknesses of the system are easily exposed by problems – be it famine, drought, conflict, or Coronavirus.

What you see when world systems break down is a return to underlying zeitgeists of what came before: the recurring cyclical nature of contraction, expansion, the rise and fall of Pareto's elites. But there is no end of history, no progress. Collapses do not take place at a particular date – for example, 1177 BC for the Bronze Age civilisation, to 476 AD for the collapse of Rome. They occur over time. The present struggle between globalised narratives and nation state assertion has been a result of the imbalance of trade and the retraction of US hegemony in the world. Like a virus, the evolution and fall of complex systems has an evolutionary intrinsic state; sometimes the collapse is exacerbated by technology. This we have witnessed by the virulent nature of Coronavirus being able to transport itself along technological lines, i.e. aeroplanes. One of the features of collapses is that, in most of them, elites had information on which to act in order to avert catastrophe. We have seen similar 'sages' or 'wise men' ignored in the contemporary world. When smoking became popular, the industry employed scientists to belittle the scientists who mentioned cancer. Science then becomes a way to silence critics. We see the same with climate change – elites manipulating agendas through 'framing' to denigrate evidence for personal profit. In societies with especially dominant elites – the UK and US, China – knowledge is circumscribed, and controlled and those silly harbingers of doom ignored or imprisoned. The delayed response to Coronavirus in the UK and the US has placed these two nations at the forefront of incompetence, due to the elites' pursual of economic motives and power. China eschews criticism for Coronavirus as 'economic interests' dominate discourses. Therefore, states have the 'knowledge' to counteract systemic collapse, but agendas and institutions are governed by financial corporations and elites. That is why the 'Plague' is not a physical one, but a plague of ideology; one which has been hijacked by a small cabal of financial interests.

The rise and fall of civilisations seem to have a cyclical occurrence. This would fall in line with religious accounts of cyclical history – for example, Hinduism and the 'Kali Yuga'. Hindus delineate 'ages' into a Satya Yuga, a Treta Yuga, Dvapara Yuga, and the Kali Yuga. The first, the Satya Yuga, corresponds with a Rousseauian state of nature; there was harmony, no agriculture, and an abundance of virtue. In the Treta Yuga, virtue falls as man discovers mining and agriculture. In the Dvapara Yuga, disease emerges and virtue declines. Internecine fighting between groups occurs. In the Kali Yuga, the final age, the environment is polluted, people pursue selfish motives, ignorance prevails. However, it is not only a religious idea. It is also a pattern of study in, for example, ecology. Here, Dark Ages occur in a cyclical manner due to ecological stress and the exploitation of natural resources. Sing Chew, in *The Recurring Dark Ages: Ecological Stress, Climate Changes, and System Transformation*,[1] argues that there were three epochs in world history he calls 'Dark Ages', which were periods after a collapse of unsustainable environmental degradation. He looks at the collapse of the Bronze Age civilisational world system and the fall of the Roman Empire, and argues that the over-exploitation of resources leads to a collapse in the system. However, this collapse is the source of a cyclical phase of recovery, and that which follows on shows a period of environmental rejuvenation. There have been three historical 'Dark Ages' – between BC 2200 and BC 1700, and one occurring between BC 1200 BC to BC 700, and one during the period AD 300, 400, and 800/900. These periods are highlighted by disorder in economic and social life. These are periods of trade contraction and movements away from urbanisation. The resolution of these conflicts needs a period of approximately 500 years for environmental reconstruction. After the Neolithic Revolution, there was a period of increased urbanisation in Egypt, Mesopotamia, and Northern India (and parts of what is now Pakistan). There began the hallmarks of developed 'society' – agriculture, division of labour, trade routes, and accumulation. Metallurgy, valleys, canals, and ziggurats indicated the transformation of nature. There then began extensive trade between the Harappans (the Indus civilisation) and Egypt. There was, therefore, a process of deforestation and soil erosion to meet the new demands of urbanised, militarised economies.

The Dark Age starting around 2200 BC through the Indian regions, Egypt, Mesopotamia, and Western Asia, was accompanied by climate change, de-urbanisation, increases in temperature, and socio-economic problems. The upturn of 700 BC coincided with the Greek diaspora expanding for agricultural reasons throughout the Mediterranean basin; this was complemented by a growth in trade routes. The Roman Empire accentuated the environmental degradation with mining, roads, and infrastructure. Again, the decline set in around AD 300/400, with the first systemic problems for the Iron Age. The decline of the Bronze Age was essentially due to the discovery of a radical new metal: iron. This crippled palace elites who had their hegemony invested in bronze. This was particularly galling for the Near East regions, who suffered in the loss of markets for bronze, tin, and copper. Power shifted therefore to iron and merchant-based city states. This followed on from the collapse of elite-based aristocracies, indicated in the move to Greek city states and new political structures. Therefore, the Dark Ages ushered in the Western Economy; with the decline of Rome came the elevation of kingdoms in Europe.

Consequently, there was a process of deglobalisation, a return to feudal relations rather than centralised ones. There was a gradual move to serf-type relations, and life focussed on manorial servitude. Our present cycle is embedded in a new 'Dark Age'. However, the term 'Dark Age', as we have seen, contains the seeds for a rethinking of the natural and cultural world. The period from the Industrial Revolution is akin to the dawning of an Iron Age; the growth in production and a 'Kula Ring' of trade, and the growth in 'fiat' currencies. What we now see is the coming of an age of enforced retrenchment for ecological and climate reasons and the corruption and commodifying of money. The periodic financial crises signal a fundamental contradiction in neo-liberal economies, with failing growth and the utilisation of financial elites moving away from industrial production and finance to 'manufacturing' money. The conflict is hastened by the realisation, for the first time in history, of real economic scarcity, especially in fossil fuels.

Economics, policy, and world governance see a competition for resources within the 'Kula Ring'. Because those resources are 'finite', the eventual degradation of capitalism will ensue. However, the spectre haunting the world is not communism but a return to archaic cyclical and decentralised power; we will see a move to the peripheries as the major powers face economic woes compounded by Coronavirus and economic shocks. Transitions to new stages are accompanied by the exploitation of resources and technology – for example, Iron Age expansion. However, technology is merely a Band-Aid on substantive cyclical processes; the Iron Age signified a feudal basis of social relations, whilst the Industrial Revolution signalled relations of wage labour. Technology *'per se'* is only as useful as the ideological superstructure of a given society and its world system. The present use of technology is geared towards a 'military industrial technological' schema, and refuses to face up to the notion of scarcity. The move out of the 'Dark Age' needs to reorient technology in line with sustainable agriculture and commerce.

The Dark Age Dawns: Existential Threats

It is a general anthropological fact that societies which are more homogenised, with varying strata and mobilisation between these levels, a pluralistic depth in civil society, economic fairness and distribution, with sustainable food production and water management, and a valuation of religiosity, have a much higher chance of survival (barring climate catastrophes). Societies which have succumbed to inherent weaknesses and fatal flaws include the Roman Empire, The Khmer, Inca and Aztec, and the Easter and Pitcairn Islanders, amongst others. These situations give us a chance, a warning, into self-destructive tendencies.

Liberal market democracy is incompatible with sustainable society due to the notion of scarcity, as we have seen with fossil fuels depletion and dependency, and the mirage of 'renewables'. The Khmer civilisation (present-day Cambodia) of Angkor Wat is a good example. The Khmer, in their ascendancy in the 1200s, were the world's largest state. The Khmer developed a sophisticated state and traded with coastal regions and, eventually, abroad. It stretched and dominated over today's Thailand, Vietnam, and Laos. However, as its population and extent grew out from Angkor Wat, deforestation occurred to make way for increasingly complicated reservoir systems for water run-off from the hills, and as population expanded, so did the extent of the schemes. The Khmer accessed timber for the construction of houses, but the local environment was damaged. Succeeding kings tried more and more technological solutions to the problems of soil damage, floods, etc, with more elaborate reservoir systems. Combined with the increasing threats of aggressive neighbours, possible climate change, and drought, the Khmer kingdom had, at its centre, a fundamental problem. It was top heavy with Kingship and inequality. The peasant class were regarded as merely the worker ants; the ones to dig the reservoirs and fight the wars, whilst the

Kings accumulated substantial wealth. Fast forward to the 1970s, and a young student at the Sorbonne in Paris notes with messianic zeal the wedding of nationalism with communism in Vietnam and attempts to roll it out in his own country, Cambodia. Influenced by Mao, Pol Pot believed in a basic form of agrarian Communism. But the defining element of the Khmer Rouge years was its viciousness; no flags at the Bastille, songs with the Zapatistas, poetry with Che by the campfire. Pol Pot's brutal interpretation of Communism was based on the Khmer peasantry's hatred of the ruling class and the centuries old animosities which this threw up. Like the Shah's Iran, it was an unequal society which favoured nepotism and the institutionalised stratification of a class society. Like the *ancien regime* of France or Tsarist Russia, the seeds of its own destruction were in the making. Jared Diamond in his book *Collapse*[1] admits that environmental factors, which he thought paramount, were always accompanied by other factors which he had not envisaged when researching the various civilisations. Here we set out to analyse the various contributions to a matrix of collapse: environmental damage, climate change, and the collapse of trading partners. The conclusion we reach is that society and international relations are involved in a sensitive Kula Ring of vulnerable cooperation.

Environmental damage inflicted by the civilisation itself is very common, as we have seen with the examples of the Easter Islanders (aided and abetted by rodents). Air pollution is one of the most striking and dangerous elements of environmental damage. In 2017 the *British Medical Journal* published an article by Robin Russell-Jones, entitled 'Air Pollution in the UK: better ways to solve the problem',[2] which provided a huge shock. It estimated that 10% of all deaths were due to air pollution. Only the Chinese have a worse record in 17%. Pollution from cars and trucks is in rampant growth – a combination of a wet, cold climate with poor levels of health amongst the marginalised poor – and you have a health epidemic on the horizon. It used to be thought that respiratory diseases were due to the climactic nightmare which Britain is, but no – it is predominantly due to air pollution. Another report in the BMJ[3] stated that deaths per year in the UK due to air pollution amounted to 29,000 people, mostly from the inner cities. Former mining areas in the UK have suffered extensively from soil contamination by mercury, which makes the soil dangerous for use. Waste from cities and towns amounts to approx. 35,000,000 tonnes per year set into landfill. This produces massive amounts of landfill gases and leachate. Leachate is highly toxic and seeps into the surface and ground water. Ameliorative measures, such as the BPEO 'Best Practicable Environment Option', shows that re-use, recycling has led to a reduction of 12 million per year. A micro impact on a macro problem.

Marine conservationists regularly highlight, through 'Beachwatch' events, the staggering amount of plastics washed up onto UK shorelines. The destruction of thousands and thousands of marine species is just one consequence of the addiction to plastics and packaging. Most UK cities are coastal, and therefore the major variable of climate change from outside makes them particularly vulnerable. We are now familiar with the concept of coastal erosion and the endemic problems of Holland, but the dreaded sea monster is now arriving in the UK. In the not-so-distant future Britain's cities could be abandoned, like Angkor Wat, and smothered forever by tidal pressures. The global pandemic of climate change is well known; I have only highlighted the micro effects (coastal collapse) which could impinge first on the UK. There is a myriad of other global concerns of climate change which most readers will be familiar with and is not the remit of this book.

External threats due to post-colonial contraction shows that history is catching up with the United Kingdom and the US. The UK, which under Margaret Thatcher trumpeted the notion that East European nations have the right to self-determination from the tyranny of Soviet oppression, was curiously myopic about events in Northern Ireland, allowing a two-tier discriminatory system to foster and grow. South African Apartheid was criticised from afar, whilst Internment without trial and atrocities were tolerated by a quiescent British media who looked the other way regarding the horrors on their own doorstep. The UK faces hostile neighbours and the collapse of the United Kingdom through resurgent Scottish and Welsh nationalism. Many of the mythic histories of nations – for example, 'Exceptionalism' – are created during times of growth, and times of success. It is only when history starts to unravel that unpleasant facts appear. Like the Roman Empire, the UK is home to a disparate group of nations searching for self-determination. On top of that, the idea of multi-cultural ethnicity, unknown to the British before the Second World War, has evolved into a dysfunctional cultural dynamic. These factors could see a return to nationalism, and protectionist single economic bloc states within the EU. The Coronavirus has shown the feeble inability of the EU to face up to any serious problems, whether it be the banking scandals of 2008, the migrant crisis, or pandemics. Pandemics expose the indolence of supra-state organisations; Coronavirus has been a much-needed boost to critics of creeping bureaucratisation of societies and the structures of 'world government', such as the UN and WHO.

Collapse or severe degradation of supplies from 'friendly' trading partners can have seismic implications. When the mutineers from *HMS Bounty* washed up on the shores of the Pitcairn Island in 1790, they found a tropical paradise gleaming turquoise blue waters, fringed with palms and soft white sand, and easy fishing from the shoals of fish which swam around the island in a kaleidoscope of colours. However, the island was deserted. After investigating the island, though, the sailors made some remarkable discoveries; they found stone temple platforms and petroglyphs, and blood-stained bones – evidence of a vanished civilisation. The mystery of the Pitcairn Islanders (and their neighbours on the Henderson Island) has only recently been unravelled – a frightening premonition of the possible fate of island populations such as the UK. The Pitcairn Island horror illustrates, albeit on a small scale, how the collapse of trading partners (i.e. OPEC, the US, the EU) can have cataclysmic effects on dependent nations. The Pitcairn and Henderson Islands are so remote that there is no organised transport to them, only the occasional cruise ship which passes by, its passengers regaled by tales of Captain Blythe and the *Mutiny on the Bounty*. What happened to the Polynesian peoples which inhabited the islands? The islands were discovered by Polynesians in about 100AD. The islands are about a thousand miles from the nearest large island groups such as the Marquesas and the Societies. Mangareva, the other nearby island inhabited by Polynesians, was 10 square miles, much bigger than Pitcairn and Henderson, but lacking any supply of stone for making tools. Better land space enabled the peoples of Mangareva to support a colony of several thousand people; they grew yams and sweet potato, bananas, irrigated by spring water, and had an abundance of oysters and shellfish. However, there was no stone to make tools (adzes) which could manufacture wooden boats. Pitcairn was a mere 2.5 miles square in size and had less resources compared to Mangareva. The population was probably only about 100 on Pitcairn; today, it supports a population of 52, a mix of the descendants of *HMS Bounty* and some Polynesians. The area available for agriculture is very small, due to the steepness of the island. Henderson is even more difficult for inhabitation, as there is no fresh water for drinking and rainwater needs to be collected; however, the rainfall is intermittent. The Polynesian inhabitants of Henderson (a few dozen) had little to export – perhaps feathers from birds or sea turtles. However, the people from Mangareva, without stone material, were able to import stone from a quarry on Pitcairn. Whilst the people on Mangareva were to a large degree self-sufficient except for stone, the Pitcairn and Henderson Polynesians had to struggle to extract a living from difficult habitat. Like today's interdependence on trade, they exchanged goods which they needed. But, in 1605, a Spanish boat arrived on Henderson, the sailors disembarked, and the horror unfolded before them: there was nobody on Henderson. Nobody on Pitcairn.

The Mangareva had deforested their island to provide farming for the increased population. The island was deforested, leading to soil erosion. Lack of wood meant no more canoes. With a surplus of people and limited resources, Mangareva gradually slipped into internecine wars and fighting over cultivable land and resources. The collapse of Mangareva meant the dependent islands of

Pitcairn and Henderson were isolated. They would have to go it alone. Pitcairn suffered from the same deforestation and pressure on resources, leading to warfare, murder, and cannibalism. The Pitcairn Islanders resorted to digging up corpses for food. The Polynesians on these islands had destroyed their environment whilst being dependent upon each other for certain essential items. If you apply this model to our own turbulent times, it is possible to see the dangers of dependency trade – the addiction to oil imports and other raw materials, the vulnerability to globalised markets, Chinese hegemony. Quite simply, the Apocalypse on Pitcairn, Henderson, and the Mangareva could become... 'Apocalypse Now'.

In *The Collapse of Complex Societies*, Joseph Tainter posits the question: why do these societies allow such collapse? Do they not foresee the problems ahead? Surely the Easter Islanders anticipated that the felling of their entire forests would cause huge problems? However, it is not that easy to foresee disintegration and collapse. Psychologists have shown that humans do not notice slow, incremental change – what is called 'creeping normality'. A collapse in community, increasing poverty, class stratification, massive levels of drug abuse and alcoholism, and the withering away of freedoms in civil society, are just some of the creeping seismic shifts in British and US culture. The other question posed by anthropologists is this: why do these societies not develop policies and methods to anticipate environmental degradation? Tainter argues that:

'One supposition of this view must be that these societies sit by and watch the encroaching weakness without taking corrective actions. Here is a major difficulty. Complex societies are characterised by centralised decision making, high information flow, great coordination of parts, formal channels of command, and pooling of resources. Much of this structure seems to have the capability, if not the designed purpose, of countering fluctuations and deficiencies in *productivity*. With their administrative structure, and capacity to allocate both *labour and resources*, dealing with adverse environmental resources is something that complex societies do best.'[4]

Tainter believes that societies have the means to cope with environmental disasters, climate change, and external shock. As we have seen, however, with the reaction to the Coronavirus crisis, centralised states, such as the UK, are top-heavy and inefficient at responding. The evidence presented here – Pitcairn and Henderson, the Easter Islanders – shows how creeping normalcy and elite accumulation obscures forward thinking. Tainter's language is couched in the paradigm of the market – he uses the terms 'productivity', 'labour and resources' – that we have the 'technological' means to combat the problems highlighted above. However, what Tainter, an archaeologist, overlooks is the political make-up of modern societies and the neo-liberal world economy. Rather than being rational problem-solving entities, modern government, in liberal democratic states, reflects the competitive elites battle for power – what Pareto noted in the early twentieth century of modern statehood. Therefore, there is no conception of the 'common good'.

Modern institutions suffer from ideological infection; structures become 'irrational'. Institutions which were traditionally problem-solving entities have now, in the US and Europe, become political battlefields of nepotism, and now, Identity Politics. In fact, modern societies suffer from an 'availability heuristic'. The heuristic (rule of thumb) belief only works in the sense that we anticipate problems which we have seen before, especially those within a few generations. This is the 'availability heuristic' – it is available for consideration, since it has happened before, i.e. periodic flu epidemics, SARS, Ebola, Dengue Fever. These catastrophes have happened before, we remember them, or we are told of them. Even so, we are grossly ill-prepared for them, due to the overriding economic apparatus. However, what modern societies do not do, and which is perhaps our singular Achilles heel, is to plan a rational response to events which we have *never encountered*. This occurs despite the plethora of scientists predicting global pandemics, i.e. Bill Gates in his TED talk of 2015. Existential threats, however, unlike the Coronavirus, may wipe out humanity. Coronavirus, whilst awful in its human impact and the death of over 2.2 million people (at the time of writing), is not an existential threat. Not only have we not prepared for 'existential' threats, but the solution to them – technology – will not help us in the long run. Technology is like sticking a plaster on top of skin cancer. Existential threats can take many forms: asteroids colliding with the earth, stellar explosions, microbes, the threat of Chinese destabilising hacks on national systems. However, some threats are greater than others – for example, an asteroid strike would be approximately a one-in-a-50 million chance.

There are three apocalyptic external threats today. Nuclear war and destruction, global warming, and the threat of artificial superintelligence. However, these huge external threats are played down, minimalised by the heuristic thinking of the elites. The Coronavirus, in one sense, could be good news for the 21st century, for it may enable us to grasp international concerns and access external threats, although this would need the devolution of powers to local players. There would need to be new nuclear agreements between the US and Russia, and a concerted scientific programme to combat viruses. Toby Ord in *The Precipice*[5] estimates that the threat of existential annihilation of human sapiens is about 'one-in-six'. This is doubly shocking if you think that in the 20th century that figure would have been 'one-in-a-million'. Why the huge change? Essentially, global neo-liberal capitalism has hastened the dangers of viruses; whilst technology, for many seen as 'neutral', has humanity staring at the cave wall. The solutions to existential threats entail a decentralising of power structures and a return to a pre-Industrial, pre-Technological sensibility and community.

Future Days

When you raise the question of 'technology', there is an immediate assumption that what you are doing is backwards; you are up against the linear, progressive mantra fed to people, and monetised through the tech giants. There is an assumption that technology is pushing us to a nirvana of sorts. There are several big problems with this commonly held view of technology. Technology is sometimes seen as a type of 'means to an end' or an extension of human activity; artificial intelligence, virtual reality, are immersive extended worlds. They are part of the human experience. We extend ourselves in a liberating way through technology. This is wrong in the sense that what technology 'is' is merely 'representations' of ourselves. It is not a question of revoking technology, but of recognising what it really 'is', and its limitations.

The closing of space and time, through technology, is the ultimate goal of technology. However, the paradox is that the more we delegate to technology, the further from the essences of humanity we become. Everything now is parcelled, compartmentalised for rationalisation – the economy, work-life, 'human resources' – and this blurs the connection to the essences. It is the process of unrevealing the essences which is more important than attempting to 'represent' ourselves through technology. And it is this 'unrevealing' that answers our original question as to the deliberate veiling of truth. Technology is not malicious in itself, but it is used to obscure. Truth is not revealed through technical or analytical thought. Essences are revealed to humankind in a variety of ways, and technology is one of them. However, in the new technological era, technology takes on the appearance of being the only essence. Technology then removes humankind from what they were originally. Technology is part of the historical structuring of the natural order, through agriculture, industry, now the net technology. Things become ordered, divided, requisitioned as part of this technological order. In space, that is land through agriculture. In the Industrial Revolution, coal becomes a part of the land to be utilised, exploited. Then tools are made from natural resources, and so on, until we have more and more modern, technological stages. This securing, ordering of natural resources continues and continues, without any inherent teleology or purpose. Nature, then machines, then people, are treated as parts of a machine.

This atomisation of the world, aptly shown through the division of labour, is reflected in the anomie of modern societies, whether through Liberalism, Fascism, or Communism. The obscuration of essence is seen in the way technology erodes space and time. Early technologies, say of indigenous communities, do not push space and time away from the viewer. Modern technologies increasingly move the viewer, through virtual worlds, away from essence. This is not the problem of technology, but the technologist. We do not get nearer to things by viewing them from afar. Technology poses a greater threat, and that is that it is *becoming* space and time, and we have forgotten the ordinary concept of being. This forgetting of existence means that increasingly, solutions to problems, seem technological, rational, and reduced. They conceal underlying realities. The solution is not technological retrenchment, as we cannot act on it, but to think on it. This recognition of technology and its dangers allows us to escape from the compartmentalising of life, of concepts, of economic or rational choices, to unveiling truth. Questions such as the uses of AI, virtual reality, space exploration, etc, are merely appendages to the central question of *thinking* about technology, of being part of the thinking, not delegating it to the technologist. For technology only works in recognisable communities, small entities where technology can be placed under scrutiny. Technology has to accord with the 'telos' of the community, not in accord with a parasitic elite. Therefore, as with Aristotle's combination of efficient, material, formal, and final causes, a combination of nature and art reveals the essences. Plato saw being as a kind of permanent presence, an historical immanence, whereas technology is merely the representation of things. Technology is part of the unveiling of the world, but just a part of it. The mistake of modernity is to place technology as the ultimate goal of society, rather than a mere representation of it, in one aspect. Consequently, other revelations of truths also take place. Space, seen technologically therefore, seems to impose a scientific, rational notion of space. So, through the Internet, an email, a long-distance call, the technological reality is that it is a linear, scientific distance over possibly hundreds, thousands of kilometres. Rationally, that is so, but to the individual essence, the space is next to him, the person could be in the next room, nearby. The feeling is one of nearness, despite the linear, scientific distance; this illustrates a social, community aspect of positive technology. Consequently, technology *per se*, is not the problem. It has been something imposed from without.

The same can be said of time. Time can be construed as a linear one of past, present, future. It is engrained in notions of progress, mechanical clocks. However, conceptions of time can be cyclical. How time flies depends on circumstance and setting. A slave's feeling of time is one of killing time. Somebody immersed in satisfying, rewarding activities, floats above time. Aristotle saw the essence of time as being the right time, the right place, the right amount. We have delegated experiences of space and time to accumulative elites, who objectify space and time, and force humankind into a narrow acceptance of it. Therefore, common sense or ordinary conceptions such as these should not be aggregated by the rationalist's stealing of space and time. For the person who crouches over a computer for endless hours has a sense that something is not quite right about their use of space and time. So, space and time are not reduced to scientific, linear conceptions of abstracted notions. They must be part of the communities, or the individual's notion of space and time. Enlightenment thought gave us conceptions as nature being exploitable, science and technology to control nature; whereas classical thought gave us metaphysical options. The description we have today, of technology, is not nuanced like this. The modern world of technology, of virtual reality, AI, etc, however, appears reminiscent of Descartes' famous 'evil demon' postulate, whereby we can't really prove the existence of the external world –whether an evil demon is running a scam on us – and the external world of cars, trees, etc, is a mirage. The virtual world *becomes* the evil demon if it is explained as the only essence in town. With technology, the idea of 'Cartesian doubt' has been thrown out of the window. As in Descartes 'cogitans' the only thing we can be sure of is our own existence. With technology even that surety is being 'delegated'.

The philosopher Robert Nozick gave the hypothetical option to enter an 'experience machine', like a virtual reality, in exchange for your present life. In this new world, you have great experiences, lots of friends, you are successful. However, Nozick maintained that you would not want to enter this pre-programmed world. What the brave new world of technology fails to appreciate is that, in the essence of things, it is the struggle, the pain, the very things which have, historically, made up our world, and lives in us in the present (and the future), is what it means to be human. The opposite, which Solzhenitsyn noted was the notion of comfort and technological escapism creeping through Western society, is what turns us weak and soporific. By delegating more and more things to technology – work, leisure, sex – we divorce from essences, and this uprooting leads to the social dissonance, community-dissolving alienation which we see in contemporary societies.

The Environment, Development, and Technology

Schopenhauer noted that a problem may often seem like a paradox but may be later viewed as a truism. A solution may seem so left-field, so off-grid, so anti-paradigm, that it seems unfathomable. Galileo, Newton, and Einstein grappled with ideas which upset accepted nuances, stoked the flames of damnation, but were seen as truisms later. Ideas such as 'growth' are still peddled by economists, despite the devastating impact on the environment. This is the problem of the neo-liberal globalised world – it appears that we have no alternative to liberal capitalism, to the 'free market', no alternative to 'liberal democracy'. The 'availability heuristic' given to the world post-Industrial Revolution is limited to the present dimension. Modern neo-liberal capitalism seems like a riddle, a paradox; it hurtles towards an abyss, but the elites tell us nothing else works. The paradox is that we need a period of technological reorientation, whereby technology, as in 'mononet' prescribed systems, is only able to work towards a moral communitarian goal, in that technology developed for weapons, security, spying, surveillance etc, would be prescribed.

Neo-liberal capitalism works like a family. There are booms and busts; crises; discontent. The happy families, though, have good structures that reconcile feuding and inequality. Unhappy families have biases, alienation, and fear. The family example can be correlated to states or communities: happy states share certain characteristics which have proven through time and tradition to breed happiness and well-being. Unhappy states or communities breed discontent and malaise. The idea originated with Aristotle's maxim in the *Nicomachean Ethics*:

'Again, it is possible to fail in many ways (for evil belongs to the class of the unlimited, as the Pythagoreans conjectured, and good to that of the limited), while to succeed is possible only in one way (for which reason also one is easy and the other difficult – to miss the mark easy, to hit it difficult); for these reasons also, then, excess and defect are characteristic of vice, and the mean of virtue; For men are good in but one way, but bad in many.'[1]

Why, though, have some states evolved in a 'happy' manner, and others declined or degenerated? The main reason scientists have put forward for the relative success of European civilisation is the environmental and geographical advantages of agriculture and livestock, which favoured the development of agricultural surpluses and then the evolution of organised states, etc. Eurasia had an abundance of hardy crops – wheat, barley, etc – whilst regions such as Africa had other crops which were more difficult to grow and in a harsher climate. Eurasians were able to domesticate animals such as pigs, horses, and sheep – they had positive traits, such as being tamed, temperament, etc, which made them easy to domesticate. These advantages led to agriculture which allowed for the division of labour; farmers would provide for food whilst others specialised in other areas – mercantilism, commerce, industry (later on). Agricultural surpluses meant increasing speciality and an increase in state-like institutions. Therefore, good governance and state institutions followed the ascent of agriculture. However, it was geographic conditions which were axiomatic. Consequently, later developing agricultural countries – for example, those in tropical Africa – have late developing institutions due to the harshness of the climate, being land-locked, etc. As Franz Boas showed in twentieth century anthropology that homo sapiens' brains are similar across continents, evolution of communities developed in different ways at different rates, but it had nothing to do with intelligence – although this myth is still peddled in the media in a subtle way.[2]

Although environmental conditions were axiomatic in early state formations; states or civilisations, within advanced societies, then fail for other reasons. Societies which fail have departed from the underlying 'telos' which made them successful in the first place. In fact, the idea of the Greek word 'telos' is paramount to our discussion. This does not mean the 'historicism' of Hegel or Marx, where history reaches a conclusion. The 'telos' of community means a recognition of cyclical truths, of a fundamental connection to nature, of community. The absence of an ultimate goal or aim of society underlines the essential archetype of modern liberal societies. Liberal democratic economies have removed 'telos' and replaced it with economic rationality, with reason. Societies with a solely narrow secular teleology will be more likely to succumb to collapse.

Ironically, however, the comparative advantage given to the Eurasians by the environment will be the ultimate downfall of industrial society. The Easter Island example provides a simple model of how self-inflicted climate change decimated an entire system. The Easter Islanders completely deforested their island and built the Easter Island statues, and at once sowed the seeds of the decimation of the people on the island. Even so, we still live in a culture of GDP and rampant consumerism without sustainability, whilst scientists and government seek *technological* fixes to endemic problems. However, whilst the Western elites stumble towards oblivion, states which succeed avoid these core deficiencies. They seek truth, seek consensus rather than privilege, develop meritocracies rather than elites, and have rational planning and specialists for experiencing external existential threats. The one common denominator in Western-developed nationhood is the restriction of the ideological framework to a self-seeking elite, through liberal democracy, which manipulate selfish agendas and issues rather than tackling root causes.

Jared Diamond, in *Collapse*, lists some salient reasons why societies collapse.[2] The main reason, going back to Malthus in the nineteenth century, is overpopulation, which leads to an increase of problems of scarcity. Overpopulation, combined with increasing climate issues, leads to marginalised communities suffering from food production problems and a collapse of sustainable development. Yet the dominant ethos is one of 'economic growth', industrialised farming, which increases, exponentially, population. Unfortunately, the discourse of politicians – the EU, the OECD, the IMF, and the World Bank – still talk of GDP and 'growth'. The GDP model is linked to the pervasive spread of the development model. 'Development' is big business – a euphemism for the expansion of contracts abroad for US and European firms, which leave small dirty ripples in the pools of Africa and Nepal and Cambodia when they leave. Beneath the veneer of 'charity' is neo-colonial paternalism. The simple fact is that development never has and never will work; a collection of white elephant projects usually unsustainable in the future, the core failure being the presupposition of 'development' – that indigenous communities in the Amazon and Tibet need Western materialism. Rajendra Karkee and Jude Comfort, in the journal 'Frontiers of Public Health', offer the following damning assessment of the entire industry of development:

'The number of non-governmental organizations (NGOs) working in Nepal has grown significantly since the 1990s due to a range of factors. A total of 39,759 NGOs and 189 international non-governmental organizations were registered in Nepal between 1977 and 2014 in various sectors, including health, agriculture, poverty alleviation, and good governance. Despite thousands of NGOs and significant amounts of foreign aid, Nepal remains one of the poorest countries in South Asia. The case of Nepal indicates that aid and donor support alone are insufficient for sustained development.'[3]

Development is a social construct, rooted in the economic and political values of donor societies. However, they do not represent the society they come from, but the elite thinking of those societies aimed at introducing Western notions of representative democracy and establishing markets for Western firms. For development projects to work, they need to manipulate the discourse of the target market. Before Ladakh was 'developed' by NGOs, the local people had no notions of 'poverty', for they measured happiness and poverty through different barometers. Norberg-Hodge studied Ladakh closely for many years; she mentions that when she first arrived in Ladakh, she was amazed by the quality of life. Beautiful houses, a cyclical seasonal lifestyle, no crime, no disease, the chemist was in the plants of the surrounding fields. When she returned eight years later, the world of Ladakh had changed:

'When I first arrived in Leh, the capital of 5,000 inhabitants, cows were the most likely cause of congestion and the air was crystal clear. Within five minutes' walk in any direction from the town centre were barley fields, dotted with large farmhouses. For the next twenty years I watched Leh turn into an urban sprawl. The streets became choked with traffic, and the air tasted of diesel fumes. 'Housing colonies' of soulless, cement boxes spread into the dusty desert. The once pristine streams became polluted, the water undrinkable. For the first time, there were homeless people. The increased economic pressures led to unemployment and competition. Within a few years, friction between different communities appeared. All of these things had not existed for the previous 500 years.'[4]

For Norbert-Hodge, the transformation of these societies results from a deliberate lie by the guardians of consumerism that indigenous cultures are inferior, and ideas of community are demonised. Sustainable development is the new catchword of the development crusade; again, a misuse of language which makes the claim that consumerist societies are in fact better than local, indigenous ones. Societies fail for a number of reasons – environmental collapse (Easter Islanders), military threats from neighbours, etc – but now the added threat is the hegemony of discourse. This is extrapolated by medias and social media; indigenous peoples become embalmed in the narrative of capitalist colonisation. Armed with a plethora of advisers, NGOs, and a missionary zeal, local elites are co-opted for financial gain to spread the good word. As in Ladakh, local traditions, housing, politics, and community, are replaced by the dictatorship of the World Bank. If you extrapolate from just that one example of Ladakh to the rest of Asia, to Africa, to the Americas... you have a concerted political and economic assault on traditional cultures and their lives – imperialism through the back door, all for the benefit of a handful of international firms and the pseudo virtue signalling of their employees.

Hence the model to be followed is not one of 'growth' but 'ungrowth'. And whilst development is often termed 'sustainable development', the environment is still destroyed regardless of the empty promises of the development missionaries. There is ample evidence documented worldwide for the collapse of environmental systems in fishing, deforestation, desertification, soil destruction, introduction of non-native species, demands for water and natural fossil fuels, to name just some. There are only limited options to stop environmental problems, to face the issues full-on. However, the current *political* structures are not conducive to facing the issues, despite the sound bites from the EU, from environmental NGOs. The neo-liberal democratic model means that essential, drastic measures, a rethinking of priorities for living, will not be faced. Hence my earlier assertion that unless there is a radical change of theory at the top, then society will head – blinded by the consumerist obfuscation – into certain destruction. Unfortunately, returning plastic bottles to Tesco will have no effect whilst China, responsible for 30% of all world environmental problems, continues to ignore the damning evidence. The Holocene Extinction, which began approximately at the end of the last Ice Age, has seen an unprecedented destruction of millions of species of fauna and flora, as well as habitats such as rainforest. The 'Global Assessment Report on Biodiversity and Ecosystem'[5] estimates *another one million species expect extinction at current rates of anthropogenic impacts.*

The current locomotive hurtling towards us is the environmental problem, and one of the solutions to this is not the exporting of the 'development' paradigm to societies living in traditionally agricultural situations. Degrowth as a solution to the environmental inferno does not entail, however, a diminution of human happiness. It means a re-evaluation of priorities, a change in the discourse of happiness, one which is not measured by Google, Coca-Cola, or Apple. The new measurements need to be community, happiness, cooperation, equality. The illusion is peddled that technological solutions, in the guise of wind power, solar power and innovative electro cars, will solve all. The degrowth alternative is not some kind of wishy-washy, 'back to nature', anarchist mantra, getting 'back to the garden' with Crosby Stills and Nash. It is actually a scientific theory based on scientific principles. In fact, it reflects the science of the 'Second Law of Thermodynamics'. A new technology makes an island of order in a sea of disorder. But entropy is increased by more than the benefit of the order. Entropy (or disorder) in the environment, therefore, is *ipso facto* a cause of environmental damage. The second law of thermodynamics states that for every unit of order made in the world, there is more than one unit of disorder. The changes in thinking at the cultural realm will enable a rethink on growth. Akin to degrowth on the material side, society needs to decouple from industrialisation. It is now becoming a mainstream idea; the 'Intergovernmental Science-Policy Platform on Biodiversity and Ecosystem Services' in 2019 summarised the need, although still couched in the 'sustainable development' model, of: 'enabling visions of a good quality of life that do not entail ever-increasing material consumption'.[6]

Connected to degrowth is its corollary – technological retrenchment. Although renewables are touted as the long-term solution to scarcity of fossil fuels, technology creates another set of problems in itself. 'Sustainable development' is still 'development' and follows the same paradigm of growth for growth's sake. A new thinking, a grassroots approach, needs to challenge the status quo. The environmental problem is exacerbated by the other myth of our milieu – the belief in technology as the solution to scarcity. In *Techno-Fix*, Joyce and Michael Huesemann outline the problems faced if you challenge the belief system of technology:

'In order to suppress anything which might threaten social cohesion or challenge the power structure, every society has taboos related to certain kinds of discourse and action. In modern industrialized societies, there is a strong taboo against challenging the faith in science and technology and their supposed contribution to 'progress'. Any questioning of that faith is seen as heresy. Those who criticize new technologies are labelled 'anti-progress' or, in more derogatory terms, 'Luddites', after the machine-smashers who opposed the mechanization of labour during the Industrial Revolution of 19th century England. Indeed, the idea of 'progress' is used to suppress criticism, to enforce passivity, and to avoid debate about the introduction of new technologies. Criticism of technological and industrial development is often stifled by invoking the illusion of inevitability, the 'You can't turn back the clock' argument.'[7]

Complex societies depend upon an ever-increasing dependency on resources for the benefit of 'efficiency'. Efficiency itself is seen as positive, value neutral, but in reality means a diminution of existing resources. The modern world faces an even larger prospect of destruction, far worse than the Roman Empire or the Mayan, through the consumption of resources. For example, the Roman society solved the falling agricultural and resource problem through empire-building and the exploitation of local resources. China is now exporting economic imperialism worldwide – the model of efficient production with cheap indentured labour. However, expanding empires come at the cost of increasing bureaucracy, armies, and social control, which are far more dangerous in modern times with the proliferation of weapons worldwide. Modern societies face similar threats whilst the language of technological 'opportunities' clouds the thinking of elites. In energy economics there is a variable called EROEI, which is represented as an equation:

EROEI = Energy Delivered/ Energy Required to deliver Energy

Current research shows that a ratio of 3:1 is necessary to utilise new technologies of energy production. Whilst some technologies (i.e. nuclear) have very efficient EROEI's, others such as fossil fuels, wind power, and solar voltaic cells, have smaller EROEI's. This means it takes far more energy to extract energy than it did before. For example, whilst at the start of the twentieth century it took approximately one barrel of oil to produce 100 barrels, it now takes one barrel to produce five barrels of oil. This stress on the exploitation of energy resulted in the collapse of the Roman, Mayan, and Khmer civilisations, amongst others. Energy resources suffer the same fate as exploiting wood in earlier civilisations; wood becomes more difficult and further away to produce and assemble, a cycle of diminishing resources which leads to collapse. It was the historian AJP Taylor who said that people learn nothing from history – the cause of wars, the causes of environmental degradation, mistakes are repeated *ad infinitum*. The media host the post-modern myth that technological solutions are available, that 'sustainable development' is the solution to poverty and hunger, that energy is there in 'renewables'. However, the EROEI figures show the increasing decline in ratios.

Energy consumption in the West is declining. This is marketed by the green environmental lobby as a reflection of the 'success' of renewables. However, the truth is that the West has now effectively outsourced energy production to China. China is gobbling up the world's fossil fuels and will continue to do so. Environmentalists point to the fact that carbon dioxide output is rising slower than the consumption of energy, but that is due to the movement from coal to gas. Hydro power accounts for 2.6% of energy consumption worldwide; wind and solar accounts for 1.5%. Nuclear power accounts for 1.7%, whilst the majority – 94% – is from fossil fuels. The only change in the market has been the subsidies thrown at fashionable renewables.

Dependency on ideas such as GDP, development, etc, only fuels the incessant demand for fossil power. The issue with renewables is that they source energy from 'low density' sources, therefore they need a lot of space. Renewables means the destruction of nature through damming, barrages of tidal basins, or the massive space needed for wind turbines stuck on hills. Then there is the hidden cost of creating renewables; it takes approximately 150 tons of coal to produce a wind turbine, plus a few tons of rare earth metals. The unfashionable nuclear industry struggles for support, although new innovations such as fusion energy – using heavy water (with deuterium) and tritium – is one solution. Research into the difficulties of fusion estimate that low temperature super conductors could provide a stream of cheap energy by 2040. It is no surprise that China, undaunted by fleeting fashions, spends two-thirds of the world expenditure on nuclear research. Like so many aspects of Western political and cultural thought, truth rarely enters the equation whilst 'opinion' and media manipulation of the consumer creates a facade of respectability which 'democracies' refuse to address.

Coal and nuclear extraction have a more efficient EROEI than Photo-Voltaic and Wind Turbine. It means that, in the foreseeable future, 'renewables' will not be able to replace fossil fuels as a source of energy. The unpleasant conclusion from the study of EROEI is that it would be unwise to move away from fossil fuels, which therefore means greater impact on the environment. Nevertheless, policymakers in government are tied to populist discourses about green fuel, etc. Even though they are aware of the low EROIE's, they perpetuate the myth for electoral reasons. The petroleum geologist, Richard Heinberg, in *The Party's Over: Oil, War and the fate of Industrial Societies*,[8] concludes that 'peak oil' is now imminent, and that politics, the war on terror, and US foreign policy, are all driven by the central tenet of fossil fuels. Therein essential change is only feasible in another paradigm. His contention is that 'homo sapiens' have become 'homo colossus', and whilst previous societies which inflicted damage did so in a world of infinite (relatively) resources, the present dimension allows no room for anything other than a serious rejection of the military-industrial complex. The boom in population and the degradation of the environment are both symptomatic of a reliance on fossil fuels.

However, the myth of technology is not only an environmental malaise; it affects people through entire generations of alienation. Place, space, and time have become virtual. There are inner-city children who have spent their entire lives within an artificial technological environment; their knowledge of 'nature' is through satellite TV, concrete housing, cars, artificial synthetic clothes. Every aspect of mass consumerism is further divorcing homo sapiens from their natural environment; the paranoia, depression, anxiety, is because we have enveloped ourselves in a plastic and concrete bubble. The manufacturing of this consent is based on the 'get happy quick' premise of urban materialism, promoted at first by print media and now through the internet and social media. Consumer goods have been shown to produce diminishing returns in almost every area; the thrill of shopping goes down and alienation goes up – you can't buy yourself out of depression. Mass production and consumerism seeps through every aspect of modern man, through dominant relations at work, civil society, and family relationships. Mass culture creates a world of fantasy, a balm for hurt minds, a temporary detour from the prison of the workplace. It breeds discontent, greed, and corruption. It produces the spiralling substance and alcohol abuse we see out of control in industrialised societies. Likewise, the process of 'mass distraction' of TV, the internet, social media, acts as a voluntary form of social control, illustrating that technology is not the positive neutral force for good represented in the media. Besides the fact that Google, Apple, etc, are unelected, they now dictate the everyday lives of the majority of the industrialised world. The modern trends of internet isolationism, in China and Russia, illustrates the vacuity of claims that the Internet was a conduit for social good; countries now have the ability to control and restrict access to the internet. Only in the dark pages of Huxley's *Brave New World* could you envisage a society which voluntarily hands over their entire personal realm to a computer, to an unelected corporation. Environmental collapse is aided by the obsession with 'efficiency' and utility in science.

The problems of the environment are rooted in the elite's domination of the economic discourse, and this discourse is 'short termism' for the benefit of economic elites – banks and industry. The complicit alliance of science and reason underlies the entire edifice structure –the gradual removal from discourse of ideas of archaic society and spirituality, of community. Modern science and technology are seen as the solve-all solution, supported by an academia and media dependent on state support and privilege. The environment and development contradictions highlighted above are based on the general underlying principle of science – that of mechanistic reductionism. By this, an analysis and understanding of the world can be gained by reducing the parts of the whole to an examination of the singular. The idea which governed the pre-Enlightenment period was one of a holistic approach to the world – to medicine, to nature. Therefore 'diseases' were seen in the framework of the whole; you cannot just focus on one aspect. For mechanistic reductionism, the human is a machine and its parts subjected to individual scrutiny. In medicine this is visible in the attempt to eradicate disease through the use of specific medicines – i.e. antibiotics, cancer cures, Aids vaccines, etc. The 'target' is the disease in isolation. The underlying causes, contradictions, and cultural issues are not seen in the whole. For example, the Coronavirus is treated as a disease which can only be tackled by finding the right vaccine. Fundamentally, the issues are more to do with man's cultural and economic practices – the abuse of animals on a grand scale, the consequences of which we have seen with zoonotic transfer. There has been a long line of Chinese-originating global scares: Sars, Swine Flu, etc. This is not merely a medical issue; it is a cultural and economic one, often induced by peoples forced to live in urban proximity to food markets. This is then connected to a political one – peripheral tributary elites of Chinese power with 'economic interests' in China will not want to upset the apple cart.

Therefore, we need to employ a holistic approach – to see technology not merely as a win-win solution to a problem, i.e. to solve dependency on fossil fuels, but to acknowledge the fact that the negative consequences of introducing new technologies into societies carry a payback. For example, the automobile seemed a perfectly reasonable solution for transport needs. However, no-one would have anticipated the devastating impact emissions have had on the environment. When, in Australia, rabbits were introduced by settlers, there was no conception of the damage to habitats that this would produce. The legacy of the mechanistic view of the world is the isolation of technology as a fix for problems which have themselves been caused by technology. The environmental and inequality issues which preoccupy thinkers will not be solved by automation. In fact, automation in the history of the nineteenth and twentieth centuries never resulted in less labour for workers or the enabling of a new brave world of leisure pursuits. Despite the hopes of economists of the late nineteenth/early twentieth centuries, the advance of automation has meant the downgrading of labour.

The human body, even at a cellular level, is dependent on a myriad of biochemical processes; everything is dependent upon everything else. This is especially true of the environment, as we have seen with the collapse of societies which tried to over-use their resources to such an extent that they created endemic problems. The modern epoch is still living in post-Enlightenment beliefs in the idea of progress – that we can improve on nature with new technologies. The idea that we can 'separate' from nature. Quantum Physics has shown that that idea is redundant. If we look at Darwinian evolution, it shows the effect of mutation and natural selection on whole populations. Therefore, certain individuals within this environment, who are best suited to it, will flourish and re-procreate. This balance is achieved through the natural selection in domestic populations. Human evolution has optimised, in conjunction with nature, a balanced environment. Nature, the world, has sorted things out over millions of years. But now, in a few seconds of time, homo sapiens have decided to control and exploit nature. The equilibrium of nature cannot be impacted without an 'equal and opposite' reaction. This reaction is visible in the extinction of millions of fauna and flora, and the destruction of marginal indigenous societies. Quantum Physics has illustrated how interconnected the world is. In fact, it evokes more the endless cycles and balance of nature; upset the balance and the wheel can buckle. The present scale of change in the environment is due to a very recent attack on nature and an attack on this balance. This analysis is nothing new; in fact, it is well known to scientists. The two laws of thermo dynamics present the problem in a nutshell. Why, therefore, do scientists continue on the road to technological paradise? Surely, they are aware of the consequences.

The problem is that we are now experiencing tangible effects of the attempt to usurp nature. It is visible; it is encroaching on the consumer, the individual. Higher prices for fossil fuels, electricity, water, visible climate change. The First Law of Thermodynamics states that energy within a system will remain constant; it can change form, but will remain in equilibrium. The Second Law states that disorder (entropy) will increase over time. Of course, these things were not of huge import in agricultural societies. The factors were so small to provoke no catastrophic consequences. With industrialisation we have the situation whereby ordered energies are extracted from the system and then returned through disordered waste materials (high entropy). It does not matter if the cars, fridges, and televisions are more 'efficient', because they are generally bigger and force more entropy. Increasing efficiency does not change the laws of thermodynamics. The modern consumer is misled by huge-scale propaganda by the green technologists. Modern economists, social scientists, scientists, speak of technology as if it were some neutral factor. As we noted earlier, certain phrases and language become elevated to heroic status even if they are falsities. The media even speaks of environmental degradation as if they were individual problems needing a quick technological fix. Climate change, soil erosion, loss of rainforests, extinction of fauna and flora, nuclear waste, human waste – they are all inter-related in a spiralling acceleration of damage. It is not even merely an environmental issue; it is the culture, the politics, the exploitation of people.

Synthetic chemicals are now shown to have been absorbed into the tissue of humans and animals, and at even small doses can affect reproductive systems like hormones. Most of the products are untested, and are spewed into nature by a few giant chemical concerns without any democratic mandate for the local people or their environment. Waste is dumped in areas where resistance is low; for example, peripheral poor nations depending on waste, etc, for jobs and income. Dukes[9] has calculated that fossil fuel carbon release is approximately 400 times the productivity of the planet's biota, leading to floods and droughts – sea level rises and the catastrophic prospect of a reduction in the thermohaline ocean circulation. A rising sea level means endangered societies for coastal and island populations within a short period of time. Husemann predicts that within 50 to 100 years the effects of climate change will be seen in the continent of Europe being too cold for agriculture. Imagine that the UK, already dependent on fossil fuel imports and gas, would be unable to feed itself. The future, without qualitative change, will see a huge impact on lifestyles, since countries will be obliged to pay approximately 50% of GDP on alleviative problems such as coastal decimation and the repatriation of huge populations to the interior. The mechanisation of agriculture also illustrates the symbiotic relationship of humans to the environment. Modern industrial agriculture has seen a depletion of agricultural workers and a movement away from traditional communities into cities. Large agro-industry now produces food more 'efficiently' at the cost of traditional rural communities. This has happened worldwide and caused the elimination of villages at a startling rate. In the US in the 1950s, the move to industrialised agriculture meant the loss of millions of family farms and unemployment. The only undoubted benefit was Woody Guthrie's' *Dustbowl Ballads.*

Technology is a very vague word to use for such a destructive force but, due to its use in the media, it has become mainstream as most people associate technology with positive things. However, technology is not merely the appreciation of the mobile phone, the car, the health developments in hospitals. For example, war and weaponry is big business. The US spends an average of 50% of the world total of a trillion dollars per year on the military, yet philosophers such as Chomsky are mocked when they speak of a 'Military-Industrial' complex. Those stockpiles of weapons need to be used; if they are not used, then there is a direct impact on manufacturers, jobs, and profit. Weapons are the main motivator of research expenditure – getting the lion's share. Technological weaponry of the modern era has produced the deaths of countless millions of people. We have also now entered the realm of the 'Health- Industrial' complex. whereby expensive technologies are used to target symptoms, again, rather than underlying causes such as sedentary lifestyle, alcohol, and cigarettes which, in themselves, are marketed through mass advertising.

The Coronavirus and the problem of viruses cannot be adequately addressed in an industrial complex which prioritises death and not life. The resources used to fund warfare could be switched to solving problems such as hunger, poverty, water, and viruses. Perhaps one of the unforeseen benefits of the Coronavirus impact will be the recognition of scientists and academics of a multi-disciplinary analysis of fundamental societal problems. Perhaps there will be the recognition of the need for scientific government. Technology, from the agricultural revolution and industrial revolution, led to a massive increase in population worldwide due to a rise in produce based on fossil fuels. With the end of fossil fuels imminent, there is the inevitable collapse of food supplies for populations. It will only be at this juncture that homo sapiens will be forced back to the farm. However, the interconnectedness of food, greed, and people, could mean endless conflicts and wars over resources. Even then, due to natural selection and the 'survival of the fittest' (a weak and technologically-dependent populace), it means that future generations of urban homo sapiens, if they have to return to agricultural work, will be at a huge disadvantage. They will be unable, due to genetically inherited weaknesses, to survive. The reason being that genetic traits from weak individuals are protected by the current environment; evolution is cruel. For example, phenotypes of people with extremely poor vision would be of no use to hunter gatherer communities, and would be removed from the gene pool by natural selection. With the advent of consumerism and the delegation of food provision to industrialised farming, people in urban centres are now completely divorced from nature. The average occupant of London lives in a small concrete space; most children's conception of nature is formed on a plastic television or on the internet. This is because technology distances the human from nature. If you think about that in the history of homo sapiens, this is a very recent development, whilst our physiology and brains have been fine-tuned as hunter and gatherers for thousands of years. We are divorced from the realities of nature. When you are close to your environment, you have to protect it – a smallholder would not pollute their garden or cut down their habitat. However, if you live divorced from reality, these things become tolerable. You are destroying other countries' habitat for those Walmart slippers, or the Apple computer.

Technology has also enabled the extraction of pre-Industrialised man into wage labour, divorced from the 'responsibility' of work. That means man is separated from the 'consequences' of work. Everything is packaged for easy consumption. The world of Fordism has been gradually tweaked in the workplace, and the ideology of 'work' becomes less visibly malign, more convivial, as outlined by Herbert Marcuse in the

1960s in his seminal *One Dimensional Man*. The modern industrial worker or office worker exchanges work for the promise of affluence; the market is an area where tolerance is pressed to the limit, nurtured by the promise of material benefits at the expense of a large degree of happiness, a destruction of community and the atomisation of family life. In all aspects of life there is this Platonic cave acting as a barrier to perception. Take, for example, the inordinate amount of time modern people spend on social media and television. The average citizen in industrialised societies spends over 3000 hours per year in front of television- time which could be used for useful social communities, sports, alternative lifestyles, spiritual pursuits, small scale farming. However, through marketing and propaganda, the masses are dumbed-down into a world of virtual reality. It is a form of neo-liberal capital where the wealthy own the companies and the medias.

Therefore, the greater problem that civilisation faces is the *existential* threat of technology to the world's population. Japan is a case in fact of the dangers of the deculturalisation of existing traditions through a destructive combination of technology and capitalism. As an island population, it offers a frightening glimpse into the self-destructive capabilities of civilisations which depart from the very telos which made them successful. Japan's population peaked in 2010. Population is declining and the fertility rate is now 1.4 per woman. The problem of low fertility rates is that it means productive age people need to contribute more to support older people. This society has produced 3.5 million people who did not marry and who continue to live with parents. 'Hikikomori' is the term the Japanese give to adolescents who remain single, living in bedsits, glued to the Internet, with little interest in sex. Almost twenty percent of Japanese men report no interest in sex. This is a cultural process accentuated by economic and technological entropy. The frightening realisation is that 'Japanification' (the alienated divorce from traditional healthy life) is an increasing spectrum of worry in other so-called 'advanced' societies.

In the 1950s, James Burnham held liberalism to be a philosophy of civilisational suicide, as it atrophies traditional and spiritual well-being in the atomisation of the individual. Marriage in the US in 2017 fell to 6.5 marriages per 1000 people; the Institute for Family Studies has traced a 'sex recession' linked to huge rates of depression[10]. The evaporation of traditional family structures, the contraction of communal and kin networks, has led to rocketing levels of angry, unhappy, and dislocated young people. Technology has replaced traditional modes of support structures, which consisted of helpers, mentors, and spiritual advisors, and led to the present milieu of social dysfunction. What made homo sapiens the successful hominid over the last 200,000 years (or possibly more) was the ability, later aided by language, to cooperate. This made homo sapiens the fearsome hunters we became. This cooperation also enabled, through mental accumulation, to pass down knowledge through generations. So, this teamwork, passed on by knowledge – each generation cooperating with a future one – has been existent for the best part of that period. This information works like a kind of knowledge bank in a living communal landscape. Now media and social media 'constructs' right knowledge, divorcing people from reality. The internet is not the source of knowledge; the source of knowledge is our family, our ancestors, those people who walked out of Africa. There are a myriad of types of knowledge: knowledge of ideas, engineering, geography, philosophy, etc. No one aspect of knowledge contributes, on its own, to success.

The expansion and inheritance of traditions and knowledge led to the gradual movement out of hunter gatherer communities and into agriculture, then state formation, etc. However, what all of this had in common, for the vast majority of the period, was the idea of community; it was axiomatic that nothing could be achieved without that sense of groupness. But now, in a millisecond of modern time, we have decided to go it alone. We decided to forsake the accumulated knowledge of our ancestors and presume we know better. The Enlightenment placed one type of reason – scientific reason – above all other forms of knowledge. A small group of Europeans, from the elites of society, attempted to reverse engineer the entire meaning of the world. Instead of community, there is the individual. Then the individual is required, by another set of elites, to exit the family because the mill and the factory require their 'time'. The corollary to this squashing of time has been technology. We are told of the wonders of technology – the car, electricity. Henry Ford would never have imagined humanity's final tab for the convenience of freedom of movement. That price we are about to discover. Technology then brings us nuclear weapons, and climate change. Now the bigger question than all of this is the following: assuming that we (or the elites) have had accumulated knowledge passed down to us slowly and surely over generations, why – in this 11.58pm moment near to the midnight of time – have we suddenly decided to implode? We are now reaching the fulcrum. The fulcrum of time means that technological progress is the enemy, not the liberator of man. It is technology, in any of these disguises, that will end the passage of mankind. But why now, at 11.58pm? The lesson to be learned is that these seismic changes to humanity have always been the work of accumulative elites. Irresponsible elites are the result of delegations. In the transition from agriculture to kingdoms, we delegated power. With the Enlightenment, we delegated knowledge. With the Industrial Revolution, we delegated freedom. With the new technological revolution, we are prepared to delegate existence.

Responses to Problems: Coronavirus, Brexit, and the Pareto Dilemma

Joseph Tainter, in *Collapse of Complex Societies,* argues that modern societies are equipped with an expert approach and planning which would defeat any crisis, and that it was the lack of qualified elites which saw the demise of older civilisations. Despite what Tainter presupposes, the efficient anticipation of change-modern liberal economies do not work like that. That is because resources are directed towards military spending and research, the centralisation of control, and the elite nature of policy decisions. Elites 'frame' issues in order to monetise issues, such as environmental policies. The Coronavirus pandemic illustrates the fact that governments worldwide were not prepared for the pandemic.

The Coronavirus pandemic was not an unexpected one. In 2014 the CHPI (Centre for Health and Public Interest)[1] in the UK stated that a flu pandemic could kill up to 315,000 people and affect up to 30 million . Yet there was no plan or facilities for such an occurrence. In a similar way, the US has been found wanting in its response to the virus. In contrast, other countries – notably in Asia – have shown remarkably good planning for these scenarios. What underlies the contrast in scenarios? The NHS – ostensibly due to rationalisation of care, central planning, and creeping privatisation – is confused about its respective roles and organisation. The study noted that vaccination systems and anti-viral distribution could not work in the present environment. The consequence of ignoring the warnings was that there were no testing supplies, not even supplies of protective equipment, and a complete lack of ventilators. In terms of policy, adequate planning would have prepared a government for scenarios related to schools, food supply, and social care. In contrast, the government winged its way and lunged from crisis to crisis as figures for deaths multiplied. Although Coronavirus is different to influenza, preparation would have saved thousands of lives. Centralised policy-making does work in top-heavy, pseudo-authoritarian government, such as the UK, but departments are uncoordinated. There has been a collapse in the confidence of the public in ministerial calibre; this is due to the lack of specialists as ministers. The UK tends to appoint 'generalists' as Ministers for government departments, who lack experience and specialist knowledge. A large percentage of British politicians have never worked outside a civil service role.

However, this endemic disease of government is a Europe-wide phenomenon, across the EU as bureaucrats occupy governmental positions. Hence the catastrophic failure of the EU to supply Europe with vaccines. In the US, once regarded as a motif for efficiency, Democrat-led towns and cities adopt the bureaucratic liberal model. You would not appoint a bureaucrat to run an entrepreneurial business or the new 5G system rolling out onto the world; you would not appoint a civil servant to organise the mission to Mars. So, why is there a tendency, in these governments, to appoint poor quality actors in important positions? The answer lies in the Pareto rule that elites 'compete' for power and consolidate their positions; the public interest takes a back seat. Also, within countries which lack a cultural and social consensus, policy is dominated by single issue affairs (minority interests, identity politics) rather than the public good. Countries which have a highly homogenous culture (China, South Korea) achieve consensus and decision-making far quicker. Within a system governed by the priorities of elites, government policy will be 'irrational'. This is because elites manipulate agendas. They frame the issues and policies to suit their narrative and economic interests. Governments attempt to 'frame' agenda akin to advertising and marketing gimmicks. This 'Machiavellian Principle of Government' is universal. However, regimes sit on a single line continuum from 'rational' to 'irrational'; good government understands the nature of framing and 'politicking', and adopts measures with this in mind. Unscientific, emotional, populist, and weak governments are susceptible to using framing to manipulate agendas.

The phenomena are well known within psychology and, increasingly, within neuroscience. Daniel Kahneman, in *Thinking, Fast and Slow*,[2] describes an experiment of neuroscientists at the University College London, in which they told subjects that they had each been given $50. The subjects were told they could then play roulette in a gamble; if it landed on white, they received the whole $50; if it landed on black, they lost it all. However, they were also given the possibility of not gambling and 'keeping' $20 – or 'losing' $30. Now, the rational actor will select either of the two, as they are the same outcome. However, the subjects were more inclined to accept outcomes which were expressed in 'Keep' terms rather than 'Lose' terms, which illustrated the irrationality of actors. The implications for neuroscientists were that different parts of the brain, i.e. the amygdala, was more active for choices with 'emotional' aspects, i.e. keep or lose. The anterior cingulate was stimulated when participants attempted to choose a more rational outcome and activated this part of the brain known for conflict/self-control.

The subject of 'Discourse Analysis' within linguistics shows how language can be abused to profit a particular narrative. As in line with 'Prospect Theory', key decision-makers manipulate framing issues. Therefore, it provides an underlying frightening moral dilemma – that our 'perceptions', as in Plato's cave analogy, have been or are 'framed' by language, by experience of moral, political codes. It proves that in the majority of cases our underlying assumptions are wrong. The current liberal democratic consensus is used as a frame to perpetuate the role of elites; it is based on government manipulation of issues. Therefore, the restriction of democratic participation is based on subjects who cannot expect to be knowledgeable about the entire spectrum of issues, from Brexit to globalisation, from real causes of poverty, development, or technology. Yet an objective detached view would posit the need for 'Philosopher Kings' and devolved power structures, localised government, rather than liberal democracy.

However, we are so engrained into ways of framing that detached objective analysis becomes obscured.

The GFC (Global Financial Crisis) of 2007 was explained and framed by the 'irrationality' of the market, rather than the incoherence of the system. The heady days of sub-prime mortgages and the speculation of bankers. However, the behaviour of the actors, as individuals, was not irrational. Using a mortgage as a financial instrument to buy a property and then resell it, was 'rational' action by the subject. The bank seller giving the loan was also acting in his rational interest – to get paid commission. The purchasing of financial instruments given a AAA rating was highly rational. The firm delivering the AAA rating makes money from that, therefore the behaviour is not irrational for the rater. Buying, then asset-stripping a company and flipping it, is not irrational for the speculator. The main problem was not irrationality, despite the focus of behavioural economists' post-2008. The main problem was the outcomes of the market. As in democracy, the outcomes are not predictable, as the main issue is the *structures* inherent in their design; it is like playing football with a square ball. The consequences of the financial speculation were catastrophic because the structural system (lack of regulation, etc) was underpinned by an ideological framework which rewards economic greed. Better decentralised, accountable structures work because local people are stakeholders in the systems.

Therefore, whilst Kahneman describes framing of irrational behaviour as paramount, in the broader world of the market it is not 'irrational'. Framing is used in areas by politicians and ideologies to convince the general body politic of public policy. It is valid in this sense, but given a structural framework and the necessary information, subjects will act rationally, but only in areas they are knowledgeable about or can participate in. The general public cannot be expected to be knowledgeable in the current structural framework. Within the current structures, democratic choices and economic choices may appear 'irrational' but are rational for the subject. This is due to the structural framework. Individuals in the current schema are becoming more and more atomised. 'Homo economicus' views his world as a private market in which he utilises his business performance the best he can, given the irrational structures. The structures which neo-liberals called 'free market' are anything but. The trend in domestic markets, and also in globalised markets, is a constant move to monopolisation and oligarchic structures. Privatisation, sold as 'efficiency', was actually the public taxpayer paying for the asset-stripping of organisations such as the Royal Mail and British Rail. The realm of the free market only exists for the dispossessed – the gig economies, the part-time workers, zero hours contracts. The atomisation of employees continues, as the structures – the trade unions, etc – exist within the logic of market efficiency, whilst the multi-national extractors of profit work in oligarchic, unregulated structures.

The market economy is characterised by fluctuations – boom and bust cycles, and ever more desperate attempts to provide Keynesian stimuli to stagnant economies. Of course, there has always been boom and bust; the Harappan civilisation which traded with the Ancient Egyptians saw troughs and peaks of trade. Tony Blair's Britain, Nazi Germany, have all used Keynesian inflations to jump-start economies. However, that model is now unsustainable due to the fundamental economic problem of scarcity; that is, the paradigm which has influenced decision-makers since the post-World War 2 period, is now redundant. Resources are over-taxed, and the cost of retrieving them more and more expensive (oil, minerals, gas, etc). The exploitation of resources is destroying habitat, fauna, and flora, at an impossible rate. Pareto, the Italian economist and philosopher, recognised the cyclical nature of elites – that liberal democratic societies suffered from economic turbulence due to the nature of the existing polity- democracy. Pareto saw society as a grand circle of elites despite the pretence of democratic regimes. For Pareto, history was 'the graveyard of aristocracies'. It was a political law that the ruling elite will feed from the troughs of the public purse; this is self-evident in the corruption and nepotism in European government, the EU, and local government. Take any small town in Europe, dig deeper, and you see Pareto's Law unfolding like the tide of history on a litter-strewn beach. The more government, the more corruption. It is a global pandemic.

The problem with elitist societies is that a few at the top are working for private gain, not for the welfare of the community. The solution, thought Pareto, was the diminution of the State, a free-market economy, and libertarian laws. Firstly, Pareto dismissed any notion that economics or democracy could be in any way 'scientific'. Like the Anna Karenina principle, Pareto saw the 'Polity' as a symbiotic whole – that the phenomena of society are not linked to one particular cause; the phenomena influence each other. One weakness, one illogical fallacy, and the edifice crumbles. Human relations and society are not 'rational', but what Pareto called 'rationalised'. This is what we saw with the 'heuristic' fallacies in the Kahneman discussions. The one constant in all societies is that a narrow elite control the majority of wealth and power: the 80-20 principle. Against this backdrop, it is easy to see how and why civilisations and empires have declined and collapsed under their own strains – that is, the collapse is due to an 'irrational', unsustainable society – although it is in the interests of the elites to convince the public that certain policies and restrictions are in the interests of the greater good. Pareto called it 'Pluto-Democracy' – the government of skilled people using public ignorance to mask corrupt and self-serving ideologies. Elites do not anticipate crises, because their function *per se* is to monetise the political sphere; politics becomes a vehicle in the race for wealth.

The miasma of Coronavirus is relatively unique to the modern era of global capital. Besides a few smaller outbreaks, we have seen nothing like it under the present liberal epoch. However, there is a contemporary allegory at the end of the nineteenth century, when a Cholera outbreak struck Europe due to the transport of the illness westwards after British conquest in the East, opening up trade routes through Afghanistan, Persia, and Russia. The industrialisation of Britain started a frantic trade with India and the Cholera Bacillus found fertile grounds in the poverty-strewn territories of India, and the new urbanised ghettoes of the UK. Cholera was part of the baggage of newly-industrialised Europe, and accompanied soldiers on the ebb and flow of revolution and war. Cholera was endemic during the Polish uprising in 1830, it accompanied the European revolutions of 1848, and was omnipresent during the Crimean War of 1853-1856. Cholera enjoys dirty, untreated drinking water. The Cholera epidemic of 1892 in Hamburg, Germany, came as another thunderbolt. This was the first 'modern' epidemic which struck a European city, so its analysis can throw light on the responses to problems which Coronavirus has faced. There are significant parallels with the present. The municipal government of Hamburg was a consortium of port-trading interests. It was the heyday of productive capitalism, with a growing industrial worker base and the problems large cities develop. Economic policy was 'monetarist', and even though Cholera was known to thrive in municipal water, the local authorities refused to allocate resources to public infrastructures. The arrival of Russian emigrants en route to the US, and the consequent outbreak of Cholera, was firstly hushed-up by the administration. There was then a cover-up and doctors were told to blame the deaths on something else. Economic policy was paramount, and elite rule meant there was no 'democratic' response to the problem. As the crisis mounted, the city was quarantined by the Kaiser, and fresh water was brought to the city using military field hospitals. The result was a clean-up of hygiene, the construction of clean water supply, and the slum clearance and allocation of social housing. The Hamburg merchant class were forced to appoint a group of skilled administrators to thwart any further costly disease outbreaks. Therefore, the crisis precipitated a 'reflection' – a look at the underlying schema of things – and hastened the realisation of reform, or change.

With the Coronavirus, we see the same miasma of deceit. The elites at first champion the economy – akin to Boris Johnson's Conservatives opting for 'herd immunity', a euphemism for *laissez-faire* complacency. Then the crisis is used to squeeze democracy; to turn 'liberal democracy' into its usual end-game: technocratic authoritarianism. These types of responses are predominant in neo-liberal economies, so we see the worst of the responses in the UK and US. Then comes the reversal. A forced recognition that some form of industrial policy is necessary, a type of decentralising to knowledgeable actors, if only for the sake of keeping the elites in office.

The Pareto analysis can also be applied to the Brexit debacle, in that the crux of the matter is leveraging power. Brexit illustrated the departure from 'norms-driven' constitutionalism- elites had finally given up all semblance of the hitherto convention that government was to provide stability and prosperity. This was caused by the neo-liberal monetisation of all spheres. Elites on either side of politics now champion, for example, in health-market forces rather than public health interest. Hence you see the massive expenditure on consultancy and public contracts. The Brexit debate saw two elites competing for power, the Blairite international euro bureaucrats focussing on inter-trade. These were essentially Remainers like Cameron and Blair, whilst the Nigel Farage, Boris Johnson nationalist section favoured an internalisation of trade and a vision of Atlantic trade with the US. Pareto divided the two types of elite into Foxes and Lions. Foxes are, by their very nature, cunning and Machiavellian, whilst the Lions are unambiguous proponents of force, the old ways. Politics is essentially the alternation between the two elites in the relentless manipulation of democracy. Plebiscites and referendums are an unpleasant interference with the elites. This was noticeable in the fact that, despite the clear result of the referendum on Brexit, the elites put their own petty parliamentary and economic interests ahead of the public, showing utter contempt for the 'democratic' process. The key to privilege is to remain in government at all costs, for to be in government – especially within the core elite of the executive (i.e. the British 'Cabinet') – is like winning the lottery. A recent article in the *Telegraph* (January 2020) newspaper noted that the combined personal wealth of the British Cabinet was 70 million pounds. Two-thirds of the Cabinet were millionaires. Civil servants have now entered the realms of millionaires.

The Pareto model is everywhere; the collusion of market and State by the takeover of public services by elites in every sector. Colin Leys, in *Market-Driven Politics: Neoliberal Democracy and the Public Interest,* shows the takeover of public services by the market, or pseudo-market organisations. He highlights two spheres – the NHS and the Media; traditional realms of public interest, now open to global capital. The pattern is repeated in sector after sector. Creeping privatisation, under the guise of the State, is the norm. The neo-liberal Brexit agenda means that the Conservative government can operate without EU prescription. The truth behind neo-liberal consultancy, whether it be in the NHS trusts or school academies, is a simple rationale: a small group of individuals gets to control the purse strings for private, massive profit. Local authorities in the UK have lost control of over 9000 schools. The introduction of 'academies' in the UK has seen schools move from local authority control to charitable trusts – again, the export of democracy away from some semblance of accountability (local authorities) into the hands of a small group of stakeholders who can pay themselves huge salaries. In a *Guardian* investigation in 2014, they showed that these academies (publicly-funded) had paid millions into private businesses, consultancies, and individuals, and there was very little accountability of public money. Pareto's elites had discovered an easy source of income – public money. There is no clearer indication of the now new neo-liberal alliance with the State. Heads of charitable trusts are gorging in the trough of public money with open abandon.

There is no conscience to suffer, because the liberal project which started under Thatcher, continued by Blair, and now has reached its apex with Johnson and Brexit, has become mainstream. Jon Moynihan, a venture capitalist, has given donations of 100,000GBP to Johnson's leadership campaign and 120,000GBP to 'Vote Leave'. He runs a company called PA Consulting, which gets the majority of its income from public sector 'consulting'... Sir Rod Aldridge, who was Chairman at Capita – another consulting and outsourcing beneficiary – gave 1M GBP to the Labour Party. The educational watchdog of educational standards, Ofsted, oversees the failure of many inner-city schools which are 'conveniently' transferred into academies. The days of the division between the State and market have long since gone. However, the elites distract public attention with divisive identity issues and increasing means to delimit realms of civil liberties and freedom. The domination of elites in British and US public life, through a clever illusion of 'improvement', 'efficiency', 'top-down' wealth creation, has meant the concentration of wealth and power in a small nomenklatura of super-rich businessmen. This type of centralised government, one with only a profit motive and with societal division as an overarching guideline, will not be able to withstand the kind of impacts which can cause collapse. There is no limit, no moral guidelines, no virtuous principle; in fact, the only principle is profit, and now that extends to health and education. Liberal democratic polities cannot act on crises, even when they are perceived by the elites. The Coronavirus debacle in the UK and US illustrates the point. In more decision-orientated societies, action is taken swiftly to stem the pandemic – for example, in South Korea. The Koreans have high expectations of their leaders, and there is a great deal of accountability. In the UK, the elitist nature of government, divorced from civil society, the myth of British exceptionalism and incompetence in planning has resulted in the worst statistics worldwide per capita on Coronavirus deaths. The Coronavirus has placed into focus the need to enlist the most competent people in positions of responsibility, rather than seeing policy through jaundiced politically correct agendas. However, the infiltration of multinational elites and capital into government is not restricted to national governments. It is also evident within supra-national institutions, such as the United Nations. For the first time in its history, the United Nations incorporated into its organisation, in 2019, an economic initiative with the WEF (World Economic Forum). Multinational companies are now part of the world political governance system – a public-private partnership of disturbing import. In July 2019, the UN and the WEF signed a memorandum of understanding so that global business would have a seat at the table of world governance. It is the 'Last Supper' for democracy. The memorandum states there will be spheres of education, women, climate change, health, and finance. However, the clear agenda of the memorandum is to give global capital a say in core areas. However, today we have a nexus of research and forecasting, computers, etc, to accurately outline potential problems. The truth is that the elites know about global warming, the rise in zoonotic transfer, about world poverty, about the destruction of indigenous habitats, the destruction of rainforests, the destruction of civil liberties and free speech... But it is not in their interests to act, for they do not have any social conception of justice. We are effectively allowing a small minority of bankers and corporations to destroy the world for private profit. Therefore, the main stumbling block is not environmental degradation in itself, but the inability of liberal free markets to face the crisis. We are often told by the media that free market capitalism is the only 'rational' system providing for the needs of people. It is one of those trite comments you hear on CNN or SKY (along with, 'Thank God we live in a democracy/free society...'). It is another example of how certain linguistic phrases become 'standardised', inauthentic. Liberal democratic free market capitalism has existed for only a few seconds in the history of the world; it is merely a recent experiment which will cause the destruction of millions of species. However, despite the evidence and an unfailing belief in 'progress', the fraudulent message from the elites means that the 'irrational' framing of policy is enforced by an accumulative elite.

The End of Democracy

The essential dilemma for global capital is that crises are increasingly inter-dependent, meaning that a slump in one area has a trickle-down effect on another because of the globalisation of markets. Although there is a tendency to pinpoint particular events in economic history – the OPEC oil price spike of 1973, and the crash of 2008 – the nature of a system requiring constant growth is that it will encounter recurring crises. This can be seen in the figures from the World Bank[1] which show a consistent fall (amidst booms and busts) in economic growth in the period from 1965 to 2010. There has also been a concomitant rise in both public and private debt (OECD National Accounts). This is set in a context of rising inequalities on a global scale. The way that modern global capitalism works has changed since the era of Keynesian inflations and the multiplier effect, which saw a boom to the economy as leading to a social balancing redistribution. This was coupled with a more 'humane' capitalism and the rise of trade unions. There were, of course, always booms and busts, but what is new in the globalisation of economies is the fact that low growth narrows margins and heaps pressure on the social market model of liberal democracy. Rising national debt has meant a reconsideration of the social market 'kind face' of capital, and the consequence has been a squeeze on public services and benefits. The new crisis is 'systemic' in nature, rather than periodic.

Despite the low interest rates of cheap money by Central Banks, economic growth has not materialised. Quantitative Easing, through the purchase of government bonds of national governments by Central Banks, has become the norm, rather than the exception. The leverage of national governments is an easier way to sustain global capitalism than the other medicine – the neo-liberal supply side model, which is unpleasant on the tongue of the urban poor. Neo-liberal deflations, supply side economics, and the control of the money supply, was tried during the era of Reaganomics in the US and Thatcherism in the UK. It meant unprecedented levels of social dissonance. The marriage of capitalism and democracy had been the leitmotif of the post-war consensus; the amelioration of the working-class into the 'system' of growth provided a social market consensus. However, this consensus is shrinking. It can be seen in the elitist representation of the polity, the contracting of voter participation, and the militancy of young, unemployed, middle-class urban Americans. What 2020 has shown is a rise in discontent – discontent by the urban poor; discontent by the disenfranchisement of swathes of American middle-class youths unaccustomed to unemployment. Civil disobedience, traditionally the reserve of the continent of Bolivar and catholic sensibilities or Third World demonstrations against dictatorships, is now a feature of most Occidental societies. Low growth, unemployment, and burgeoning social and cultural problems, have tested the patience of peoples frustrated by a dislocation of democracy and a removal of free speech.

The Coronavirus shock has highlighted the end of 'Parliamentary Democracy' and the confirmation that Britain has always been, since the Lloyd George removal of the House of Lords veto, a 'Parliamentary Dictatorship'. In the UK, there is no 'separation of powers'. The Judiciary is an increasingly politicised arm of the civil service. Real power lies with the executive. A majority in the House gives the main executive *de facto* jurisdiction over the country. It is not surprising that a Prime Minister can take advantage of the British Parliament's annual proroguing of the House of Commons, to introduce wide powers of law enforcement and restrictions on liberties. The truth is that the UK 'democratic' system works through the powerful remit of an executive body akin to the 'Committee of Public Safety'. Robespierre would have fitted in nicely, if it wasn't for the total absence of calibre within the cabinet.

The UK Prime Minister does not answer to a written constitution, as does the President of the US. The House of Lords worked as a bulwark against parliamentary excess; without it, we had the obsessive politically correct legislation of the Blair years.

Consequently, the 'Terror' was unleashed on a quiescent British Public, weak and strangled by years of totalitarian legislation, which reached into every aspect of family and civil society. The British State has unheard-of powers to remove children from families, even at birth. The recipients of the terror are largely poor working-class families, unable to offer resistance, abused by fee-earning law firms. Men in the UK have been suffocated by the incessant movement of rights away from men to women, often losing even basic rights to their children. The realisation of the import of such a suffocating civil society, unheard of in Islamic countries, is now crystal clear as the UK executive removes even the last vestiges of personal freedom during the Coronavirus debacle.

In the UK there was the bizarre spectacle of various tiers and mass exoduses, as if from Phnom Penh, as people escaped to the periphery. That thousands of people were standing together in train stations meant that the new strains of the virus were able to spread their wings as well. However, what Johnson and Neil Ferguson) knew was that they would copy the Confucian terror of the Chinese. However, the Chinese at least don't try to pretend they live in a democracy, and have convinced their people that technological freedom is more important than real freedom. In Britain the flagbearers of the establishment, the BBC, still unashamedly trot out the 'we live in a democracy' caprice. The difference between the Chinese and the British approach to the virus reveals titanic levels of incompetency in every aspect of British government and the Civil Service. Ferguson reveals the metropolitan elite's contempt for ordinary British people. In an interview with the *Times* newspaper, he claimed that the Chinese had enabled a 'medieval' lockdown response to the crisis and wanted to copy it:

'as infections seeded across the world, springing up like angry boils on a map, Sage debated whether, nevertheless, it would be effective here. 'It's a Communist, one-party state,' we said. *We couldn't get away with it in Europe*, we thought. And then Italy did it. And we realised we could.'

This grey and murky world of democratic accountability is visible in the lack of transparency as government is more and more outsourced and invested in undemocratic agencies and institutions. There has been in the US, for example, a dissipation in the standard-bearing flag of the 'separation of powers'. This was stated by John Adams in 1779 in the Constitution:

'The legislative department shall never exercise the executive and judicial powers, or either of them: the executive shall never exercise the legislative or judicial powers, or either of them: the judicial shall never exercise the legislative and executive powers, or either of them: to the end it may be a government of laws and not of men.'[2]

The idea of a resolute separation of powers should enable the rule of law and allow identification of the rule of men; that is, who is responsible for what. The doctrine in the US of 'non-delegation' meant that they could not delegate law writing to agencies. The plethora and growth of agencies pushes government away from the public; it filters policy away from democracy and accountability. In the US, there are now 300,000 federal crimes, 98% of which have never been passed by Congress. The politicisation of the various arms of government means a larger unaccountable elite.

The calibre of Democratic politicians does not bode well for the future. Kamala Harris claimed she would ban assault weapons by 'Executive Order', to which Biden was forced to admit was not in the power of a President and they would have to 'follow the Constitution'. Whilst an Attorney General in California, she attempted to criminalise 'climate denial'. Kamala Harris, the Vice President of the US, is ignorant of even the basic workings of the American political system, claiming that states require clearance by central government *vis a vis* abortion law. They do not, but her anti-Catholic bigotry and fanaticism clouds judgement. The dissolution of the separations, and the growth of bureaucratic institutions, has cast a shroud of insincerity and dishonesty across the face of government. It means unelected quangos rule much of state and civil society.

Voter participation at elections is notoriously low. Since the introduction of universal suffrage in the UK there has been a consistent decrease in the number of voters at general elections. From a peak of 84% in 1950, the fall has continued. In the election of 2001, Tony Blair was elected with a 59% turnout. The election of Ronald Reagan in the US saw a turnout of a quarter of the population. In elections, personalities aside, there cannot be any other explanation for this long-term trend, other than voter apathy. It is even more apparent with younger voters; a drop-off at a remarkable rate. Perhaps it is because young people feel that 'democracy' or the political nomenklatura do not reflect their thinking. My contention is that young people, with the advance of the internet, technology, and virtual worlds, etc, are expressing themselves 'outside' of the system. Not in the sense of the hippies and communes, the 'off grid' communal movements, etc, but a fundamental turning away of traditional models of democratic participation. The younger generation, with more access to knowledge away from traditional media outlets (i.e. BBC and Sky News, CNN) can form their own mindset. That mindset is 'extra-political' and can see contemporary politics as merely an extension of elite power and influence. However, as I will argue later, the technological solution, the original freedom of the Internet, also has a cost which is part of the paradigm. In the US and Canada, the trend is similar to the UK. The *Halifax Examiner* in Nova Scotia report in 2017 shows a decline in voter participation from a high of 82% in 1960 to a low, in 2013, of 58%. The solution, some say, is to force the people to vote, as in Australia. One-third of US voters do not know the name of one of the three organs of American democracy, only a quarter know the name of their senator. There has been, and still is, a long line of dissenters, who argue that democracy, in its representative form, is inefficient in arriving at democratic outcomes. It appears that whilst advocates are clear about the 'processes' or technical form of democracy, from ballot boxes to electronic voting, they are not clear about democratic outcomes. That is: do we really desire an outcome which is itself undemocratic and inefficient – for example, the stalemates of proportional representation and coalitions? Therefore, there has been an historical evolution of ideas which attempt to tamper with or reform the representative model.

John Stuart Mill, in the nineteenth century, favoured giving extra votes to university-educated people and those in intellectually difficult jobs. In 1855, Connecticut introduced a literacy test for voters which was later rolled out to the whole of the US. This allowed the US to circumvent the Fifteenth Amendment by restricting the votes of blacks and immigrants. This qualificatory system was only abolished in 1975, whilst the US held itself up as the guiding democratic beacon of the world. We need to move participation back to the people and to decentralised regions. Direct democracy, feasible now through the internet, would allow for more access to the executive arm of government, devolved to local areas. However, European culture is so engrained with cultural notions of 'representative democracy' that the idea is sullied by the elites in their fear of the *'sans-culottes'*. Real democratic participation and the deregulation of civil society through the Greek idea of *'parrhesia'*, or fearless speech, in all realms would also invigorate the political world. The contemporary lurch to 'identity' and 'gender' roles has divided homo sapiens; used by elites to push democracy away from working class people. David Estlund, in his book *Democratic Authority* (2008), argued that democratic procedures are fair and that they produce good outcomes. You could argue that democracy is 'fair' in the sense that it gives everyone a vote. My contention is that there is no evidence to suggest the present democratic system produces good outcomes; in fact, the democratic process handicaps public policy, delays outcomes, breeds corruption by allowing elites to manipulate what is actually 'on' the policy agenda, and leads to an endless circle of single-issue dramas. For example, you may vote for your local MP but have no say in whether this MP agrees to selling arms to Saudi Arabia, leave the EU, bomb Iraq, endorse the trade deal with China despite human rights abuses (irrespective of the virtues /demerits of those things). Once the MP is elected, he/ she is effectively divorced from the body politic. In this vacuum grows all the issues of bureaucracy, corruption, and nepotism which democracy facilitates. So, democracy may 'appear' to have fair procedure, but it is the outcomes of democracy that are plagued with problems. From an anthropological standpoint, it could be argued that democracy is culturally relative to the prevailing epoch, of liberal political economy, just as the Aztec tradition of mass human sacrifice appeared entirely rational to the Azteca or the felling of their entire habitat was rational to the Easter Islanders. However, would it not be better to make the system so democratic that it 'guarantees' better outcomes? You descale down, devolve power, not to large cities but to small clusters of communities. Everybody is responsible for public policy – not civil servants in London.

The 'populism' of De Tocqueville (we could say 'the general will') is not to be confused with the term which, for example, is used to describe the right-wing supporters of Trump, etc. Definitions of right and left no longer describe the complexity of the modern polis. The 'Liberal Order' has drawn into its ambit a larger and larger sphere of working-class and middle-class people who have benefitted *vis a vis* the public sector inflation, University access and 'manufactured' jobs in a swathe of charity, academies, think tanks, and other publicly-funded entities. Organisations such as the BBC personify the new group. They are supported by a large technological elite, likewise divorced from precarity by the domination of this sector and its global reach, which means low taxes, high income, and share dividends. The new 'Populist Order', on the other hand, consists of disenfranchised groups drawn from a caucus of anti-elite, religious, private enterprise, entrepreneurs who dislike the new dominant liberal ethos running through Western society. They have nothing to gain from public indebtedness/taxation agendas, and many have a spiritual dislike of 'equality' modes of thought, political correctness, etc. This group note that the deliberate public indebtedness required to fund the public sector, universities, etc, works through rewarding wealthy elites who benefit through the guaranteed pay-outs of cheap government bonds. Whereas before, the wealthy would have been opposed to indebtedness due to inflation fears, they now have easy access to public money.

Rather than progressive taxation, which was the default option of the 70s/80s, the new veneer of liberalism indebts itself at the expense of public sector borrowing. Therefore, the new technocratic liberalism needs to engineer the consent of the traditional third bloc (populist order) through media manipulation, behavioural psychology, and a police force more and more drawn into ideological roles rather than crime. The Coronavirus episode has been a brilliant opportunity for the further attack on the populist order, and a drawing down of liberty, as the UK, Europe, and the US move towards further control over societies. Modern liberal government has become the 'Committee of Public Safety'. As in the French Revolution, the liberal order needs to appeal to safety and health, as in a plague, to assure conformity. Here, it is the alliance with the anonymity of technology, invoked as neutral, we delegate to technology, to the expert. It is an old ploy, the spectacle of the pestilence, the 'Pogrom' (Jews as a disease), to divest power away from people, but we allow them to have bread and circuses.

De Tocqueville could see the dangers of populism or 'the tyranny of the majority'. This populism, however, is now the liberal order mentioned above. Consequently, he believed in a stew of democracy and aristocracy; a major theme of his was the concept of 'greatness' within democracy, for he feared that the equality of Locke, for example, emphasised only mediocrity. De Tocqueville gave the example of the attitude of the medieval nobility to kings; one of heroic resistance. Tocqueville emphasised, in the private realm, notions of self-restraint. The individual, within the body politic, should enjoy the benefits of materialism. However, De Tocqueville would never have thought that individuals are obliged to follow social movements such as feminism or systemic racism. Virtue should be tempered by pride in one's own soul. Merely 'self-interest' leads to the tyranny of the majority and the submission to a type of 'woke' conformity. Therefore, individual rights are best achieved by oneself; it is not for government to 'dispense' rights – it is for government to 'protect' the rights of individuals from the mob. What is seminal to the present debacle in the US is the falling back to a myopic belief in the dualism of Rousseau; at once a libertarian self-love and unbridled materialism with the collectivist and unfree coercive state. There is a huge paradox on the new cultural left: that is, the belief in selfish autonomy in most things (i.e. abortion) whilst needing an authoritarian coercion of opponents (cancel culture) to achieve social reforms. The liberal left see their intellectual heir as Rousseau with his ideas of the 'general will', in that man must be 'forced to be free', in that there is really, deep down, a shared consensus. The general will, however, is an abstract, and needs the effective separation of powers and a vibrant civic culture to prosper. Without moral and material restraint, without community, without respect of others, there can be no Rousseauian utopia.

That the French Revolution soon descended into Dante's Inferno was not missed on De Tocqueville. The 'Committee of Public Safety' is now invested to the general will of the tech giants and social media. Non-believers are shut out, lose their positions, need to be re-educated. The general will of Rousseaau was not tolerant to entities competing with the State within civil society. The Church, community groups, the family, see moral authority moving to one of self-absorbed materialism and a collective general will of thought. Representative democracy means the 'division' of society, as in the US and UK, into partisan groups – winners and losers. Real democracy allows competing ideas, on a level playing field, with fair participation for all and their opinions.

Populism and the Economy

Concomitant to the eclipsing of democratic ideals is the effect this has on political economy. Democracy aids the proliferation of populist government to the extent that it also enables the erroneous use of public debt. Crises enable the expansion of the Leviathan; through financial, surveillance and police measures. Powers sequestrated during crisis are never relinquished. The tendency is that a crisis allows the proliferation of public debt; at the end of World War II federal spending in the US was 11.4 per cent of GDP. During the financial debacle of 2008 this figure surpassed 20 per cent. In 2020, the proposed $1.9 trillion stimulus is set to dwarf these figures. Semi-emergencies prop up government by irresponsible spending and debt; they aid the dialectic between populism and voter as government promises easy cheques to dependent groups. Periods such as the 'New Deal', the Covid stimulus also embolden 'economic nationalism' as public sector and home industries get the lion's share of financial support. However, the populist expansion is a contraction of democracy and freedom: the state becomes more of a Leviathan and the people more dependent. Populist government, therefore, buys the support of voters and indebts the community. However, Wolfgang Streeck maintains that the period of 'quantitative easing' has also coincided with a contraction and not an expansion of democracy:

'Growing public indebtedness is put down to electoral majorities living beyond their means by exploiting their societies' 'common pool', and to opportunistic politicians buying the support of myopic voters with money they do not have. However, that the fiscal crisis was unlikely to have been caused by an excess of redistributive democracy can be seen from the fact that the build-up of government debt coincided with a decline in electoral participation, especially at the lower end of the income scale, and marched in lockstep with shrinking unionization, the disappearance of strikes, welfare-state cutbacks and exploding income inequality. What the deterioration of public finances *was* related to was declining overall levels of taxation and the increasingly regressive character of tax systems, as a result of 'reforms' of top income and corporate tax rates. Moreover, by replacing tax revenue with debt, governments contributed further to inequality, in that they offered secure investment opportunities to those whose money they would or could no longer confiscate and had to borrow instead.'[1]

Governments, therefore, were replacing the depletion in taxation revenue with public debt. The shortfall in revenue is blamed on this accumulating debt, and is sold to the public in the form of the necessity for cutbacks and the type of privatisation of State sectors in education and healthcare. Government debt in industrialised countries has increased as a percentage of GDP from approximately 40% in 1970 to approximately 90% in 2010[2]. The period has also seen a movement away from national policy-making to centralised institutions such as the ECB. The merger of the State and market capitalism has been the predominant feature of this period.

Despite the inefficiencies of the State, capitalism as a *modus operandi* continues with its emphasis on consumerism and a culture of mass media participation in commodification and deliberate marginalisation of radical or spiritual alternatives. However, the sunset of participatory democracy, as evident in the Asian model, is now replicated in the West and is likely to follow suit with increasing squeezes on democracy. Karl Polanyi[3] set out the three 'fictitious commodities' of capitalism – labour, land, and money – and asserted that these three commodities were not 'real' commodities, and they were held back by regulations in the marketplace; i.e. trade unions in labour, environmental concerns to land, and the commodification of money. The commodification of money, the deregulation of the financial markets, led to the collapse of 2008 with the availability of cheap loans in the mortgage market, etc. World capital has also reached a hiatus in the sense of restrictions in land (natural resources) due to the economic notion of scarcity – the finite availability of land and nature to exploit. The technological 'green' solutions posited in the media are merely attempts to circumvent the obvious. Labour has seen its traditional safeguards eroded with the dismantling of trade unions and the adoption of traditional socialist movements into mainstream politics (i.e. the British 'Labour' Party). The main motives for repair – i.e. the EU's free movement of labour – were convenient tools to supply immigrant labour for Western economies, meaning degradation of wages and conditions for indigenous workers in the UK, France, etc. However, with the potential break-up of the EU and the rise of 'traditional populism' across Europe, the expanding market of labour flexibility has hit the buffers. Therefore, the three commodities of capital are fast approaching exhaustion.

Nevertheless, there is the apparent contradiction within capitalism that, despite the above three provisos, consumption of material goods seem to continue unabetted. This is down to innovative R and D, and endless marketing and advertising. However, there may come a point where homo sapiens realise that they have achieved the material aspects of Maslow's hierarchy of needs, and contemplate the disconnect between materialism and happiness. One of the contradictions of neo-liberal capitalism is that it requires growth; we are now near to the limits of growth. Is there an endless technological ability for production to reinvent itself, to create new needs? With private and public debt levels where they are at present, it would appear that capitalism has reached its zenith in the West. Even close to zero interest rates do not appear to correct growth slowdowns. This reflects the Keynesian analysis that inequality means low growth and a desire by capital to seek speculative investment solutions to this problem, i.e. using the cheap money from central banks as investment opportunities. The end of history has been turned on its head for those apologists for the liberal market, such as Fukuyama; those who predicted that historicism means liberal democratic markets. That hope is in tatters as capital reaches growth limits. There is a contradiction inherent in the model: that is, that the oligarchic greed which sits at the top of society may cause its downfall from a disenfranchised people who are being squeezed for more cheaper hours in unregulated labour. The bloated public sector is unsustainable. In the previous Keynesian economic model of the post-war period, there was the supposition of 'trickle down' wealth, the idea that profits were reinvested and wages would rise to satisfy worker discontent. Now what I term the 'Oligarchic Model' of capitalism sees money gushing to the top, with this method increasing in Europe as elites realign to the new global markets. Therefore, these countries suffer from deep inconsistencies. The oligarchical survival of this type of capitalism is only maintained through political and technological repression and surveillance, a curtailing of genuine participation in civil society. Therein lies the Trojan horse of global capitalism, for it will, sooner rather than later, be humbled by the realisation of ordinary people to simply 'opt out' of the system. The rumblings of the storm can be seen in the protests in the US.

The fundamental mechanism of global capitalism can be represented by the equation:

$$r > g \quad \text{This states that r= return on capital}$$
$$\text{and g= economic growth/social income}$$

This feature was a constant one since the onset of the industrial revolution, and led to more and more inequality. This was subsequently constrained by social and labour movements in the twentieth century, progressive income, and inheritance tax. This was an ideological construct; it was fought and won by labour movements in the age of 'trade unions' and socialist movements. The opposite of this – the paradigm of the 'new right' after 1980 – was that the free market was the regulator of economic thinking; it was presented as a 'natural' equilibrium. This was aided by the tendency within academia, especially in economics, for mechanistic reductionism – of studying a subject in isolation of other aspects or other disciplines. Most societies in history produce elaborate apparatuses to justify inequalities: the gods of the Aztecs; the hierarchical society of the Khmer and Angkor Wat; the caste system of India; the Protestant work ethic. The modern system of

Oligarchic Capitalism uses the ideology of the free market to state the 'natural' nature of inequality. Modern neo-liberal capitalism rests on the premise of a continuation of the Adam Smith-type of 'natural' free hand of capital. This, however, was an ideological rather than an economic construct, although *The Wealth of Nations* was ostensibly about economics.

Each capitalist epoch has its own mechanism of justifying inequality. During the era of Reagonomics, that justification was Hayek's *Road to Serfdom* – a call for free markets, and the disappearance of the hand of the State and regulation. The central premise of these justifications is that inequality is a natural phenomenon. Thomas Piketty in *Capital and Ideology* argues that inequality is a social construct rather than a deterministic one:

'Whether I talk about Sweden, India, France or China, I try to show that the level of equality or inequality is shaped by socio-political mobilisation and ideological changes, rather than by permanent and deterministic factors.'[4]

Piketty outlines the nature of 'proprietarianism' – that modern societies have been structured around the premises of the *ancien regime*. That is, the tripartite division into nobility, clergy, and commoners. Each component of society performed an 'ideological' role. So, the nobility organised law and order, and the Church offered spiritual solace. The commoners accepted these ruling ideologies, but dissenters gradually developed a buffer to it from the Industrial Revolution onwards. However, the premise of society, although couched in egalitarian language, was still essentially proprietary for the ruling elites; all people were officially allowed property rights, but the reality was that only a small section inherited legal access to property. Therefore, it was only a 'legalistic' attempt at equality.

The twentieth century saw a burgeoning increase in progressive taxation regimes and a more equal distribution, combined with access to education and health. Piketty, therefore, points the way to increased progressive taxation as the solution to alleviating inequality. Although Piketty's analysis offers a broad sweep of history, the study fails to appreciate the alliance of State and market which has become an increasing feature of modern neo-liberal capital. A minority section of the 'working-class' of most European countries have been co-opted into the mantle of the bureaucracy and the EU. This has led to a fundamental reduction in the power of the third bloc. This is a salient point. For the common misconception of the elites, especially on the liberal left, is that the working-class have gone 'nativist' and aligned themselves with nationalist parties or 'populism'. In fact, the assumption is that the working-class is inherently 'racist'; that they are beyond reforming. It is the epitome of a kind of elitist social Darwinism, but, in fact, it completely misunderstands the nature of working-class discontent. The crux of the matter is related to the wedding of the State and market mentioned earlier. Piketty defines two elites: one he calls the 'Brahmin educational elite' – those typically drawn from the liberal metropolitan elites; and the other, the 'Merchant elite' of business, who orientate themselves to the neo-liberal global capitalist model. Both of these elites are increasingly drawn to 'extra-national' allegiances – the Brahmin left following 'global' liberal issues such as gender, rights, etc, through a dumbed-down globalised social media, the 'merchant elite' through the economic promises of globalisation. The two elites mentioned have very little interest to the traditional working-class voter, although they have co-opted a few into the State apparatus. This leaves a huge portion of working-class people who feel disenfranchised on a political level and marginalised on an economic level.

The Labour Party in the UK, Democrats in the US, exemplify parties which appeal to the State-entrenched civil servants and the middle classes of the metropolitan elites. They have either lost or deliberately sacrificed their traditional base because *they have never delivered on inequality issues.* The new strategy is to divide the third bloc by accentuating race issues, identity politics, etc. The weakness of democracy and populism is that it draws people away from the essence of real problems to fight soft issues and single-issue political struggles. The OECD figures shows wealth moving to the elites – the top 10%; inequality has grown in almost all European countries from the period between 1985 and now: OECD graph Inequality[5] (see Appendix 1)

This, despite the purported social policies of the EU and the so-called 'third way' of social democracy in the UK with Tony Blair and the Equality Act. The mantra of the EU and the metropolitan elites has now been abandoned by traditional 'nativist' working-class communities. The model is replicated in the US where, in regions such as Kentucky – devoid of employment and the collapse of traditional models of agriculture – there has emerged a kind of 'lumpenproleteriat' who are of no interest to mainstream political parties. The abandonment of these communities by (ostensibly) Labour parties means they will pursue activities which the mainstream metropolitan elites find offensive – a revaluation of the benefits of patriotism, community, and family. They will become an entrenched bloc against liberalism. The media in 2020, before Coronavirus, was full of articles on 'Poverty Increasing', 'Child Poverty Increasing', etc. The assumption may be that this spike in poverty was a result of the Coronavirus. However, as the graph shows, it has been an omnipresent for a long time. In 2017, child poverty was up again – every year since 2010. The UN report on Poverty in Britain shows a society suffering by massive inequality and child poverty, caused by austerity measures and the culture of a country which institutionalises class distinction. The Equality Act has had no effect on poverty in the UK. The report criticises the 'punitive' and 'draconian' Universal Credit system for failing to provide for poor people. Reductions in council funding has produced the closure of the traditional tenets of a community – libraries, youth facilities, etc. Likewise, the introduction of technology as a means to distribute Universal Credit has resulted in the disenfranchisement of millions of poor and old people. The levels of homelessness, suicide, poverty, and food banks, stands at odds with a country which is the fifth largest economy in the world.

The author of the UN report, Philip Alston, portrays a British society broken and poverty-ridden:

'After visiting towns and cities including London, Oxford, Cardiff, Newcastle, Glasgow and Belfast, Alston said that "obvious to anyone who opens their eyes to see the immense growth in food banks and the queues waiting outside them, the people sleeping rough in the streets, the growth of homelessness, the sense of deep despair that leads even the government to appoint a minister for suicide prevention and civil society to report in depth on unheard-of levels of loneliness and isolation".'[6]

The last point is indicative of even a greater malaise in Britain. Whilst we so far have focussed on the legalistic means to restrict debate, the disastrous social policies of both Labour and Conservative governments, growing poverty, and social problems, the cause is not only "austerity' and cost-cutting by the UK government, but a prejudicial inflation of a public sector to co-opt a section of the working-class. Preferred groups such as the Police, the Army, civil servants... groups which 'implement' the policies of the metropolitan elites depend on increasing indebtedness by government, which is unsustainable. Unfortunately, populism encourages, as we have seen, the escalation of the public debt. The public sector versus the private sector is a salient feature of modern Britain and the US – another fault line of division. OECD figures show the number of public sector employees as a percentage of the population. In 2013, the UK had 21.5% of its total workforce working in the public sector. This figure is trumped by only former Soviet countries (Russia at 40%), the Bahamas (at 33%), and France (28%). The Japanese (normally a motif for efficiency) have 10% of their workforce working for the State – less than half of the British model.

However, besides the evidence for the dysfunctional nature of British society, compounded by the mess of Brexit, lies a more general malaise. It was touched on by Philip Alston in his UN report when he mentioned loneliness and isolation. When Marx spoke of 'alienation', he was writing at a time when the traditional working-class were involved in Lowry-type industrial landscapes; the new changes to society are not the materialist nightmare which Marx painted. We now have, unforeseen before, a new marriage of convenience – the State and the market – but all at the expense of the individual and the community. In advanced liberal democracies there is increasing alienation from traditional schemas. Hence the appeal of populist parties across Europe, including Le Pen in France, Urban in Hungary. For, despite the mantras of the metropolitan elites, appeals to poverty, tradition, democracy, and community, do resonate with ordinary people. Countries such as the Czech Republic, Poland, and Hungary have much higher of levels of participatory civil liberties than does the UK. The intrusion of the State into family life would be anathema to these and Islamic societies, for the body politic is limited to the State and not the family. The contention of this book is that not only is globalisation a cause of the Coronavirus disaster, but that inequality is its pernicious partner.

Historical analysis shows that pandemics are far more common in times of 'anomie' and gross inequality. This model can be extended outside of Europe. Poverty has a direct influence on the Third World and now, more and more, First World health. The neo-liberal model means the exporting of norms to 'developing' countries. Increasing numbers of 'wet markets' and the encroachment of poor city dwellers on the countryside means poverty leads to poor health and viruses. Increasing poverty leads to debilitating health. The BMJ (British Medical Journal) outlined the issues:

'At the heart of the poor state of health in Africa lies a failure to tackle extreme poverty. Today, 46% of the population live on less than $1 (£0.55; €0.82) a day, a greater proportion than 15 years ago. The failure to tackle poverty is due to several inter-related factors, mainly economic stagnation and the related debt crisis. Support from the International Monetary Fund and World Bank for countries with crippling debt has been contingent on governments adopting painful structural adjustment programmes. These have required countries to put strict ceilings on government spending in the social sectors, limit public sector recruitment, and liberalise trade.'[7]

Following the 2008 economic crises, there was a flu epidemic in the UK in 2009. What few realise is the social stratification of victims showed that death rates were three times higher amongst the poor than amongst the rich. Coronavirus has shown a disproportionate death toll on black and working-class communities. This is directly related to poor economic status and health care. The nature of pandemics such as the Coronavirus is that it economically highlights stratified inequalities. We have seen research evidence that suggests the Coronavirus impacts low-income groups, who are more likely to be laid off, especially those in the gig economy, and part-time workers and those in the 'business end' of the market, rather than the civil service who have longevity and security of contracts. The public/private trend will be exacerbated by the current pandemic, leading to social unrest due to disenfranchisement of the precarian groups. Indian migrant workers illustrated the precarious nature of marginalised groups and the shocking number of deaths of people retreating to the countryside during the pandemic. Precarious workers are also more likely to take risks during a pandemic, and continue working in poorly regulated risk economies. The World Bank has even accepted the mantra that reducing the rich-poor gap is beneficial to the economy, although the current global economy of growth has only worsened this process. The lack of real democratic participation, a myriad of undemocratic institutions and agencies, populism and inequality, has meant a seismic distrust of the governors by the governed. A group of elites have attempted to dismantle, through the squeeze on democracy and the corrupt use of public debt, age-old conceptions of democracy and 'truth'. In this there is an attempt to change the essential truths of existence.

PART 2
The Strange Death of Truth

The History of Truth

In *Human All Too Human* Friedrich Nietzsche maintained that 'Convictions are more dangerous enemies of truth than lies'. The usurpation of truth by the imposter 'conviction' is all too common in the modern world. Media news and the Internet – the main fountains of knowledge – provide a constant stream of simplified, dumbed-down items. As psychology research shows, i.e. Kahneman in *Thinking Fast and Slow*, intuitions and convictions belong to the first type of thinking: impulsive. Most intuitions, convictions are based on the 'availability heuristic' of what has passed before or is available. Regardless of nuance, it fuels the binary thinking of the modern era, precipitated by the unedited realms of social media. The second type of thinking – slow thinking – reveals a more contemplative approach, where thinking takes in a lot more evidence and nuances than the random.

We are now in the age of conviction – the first way of thinking. Unfortunately, this is a bad way to arrive at a valuation of truth. What passes for 'truth' is merely convictions, intuitions or, even worse, agendas. It was Heinrich Heine who wrote that thought precedes action. It was Heine who foretold in 1834, as poets often do, the forthcoming of the barbarism of the Nazis. He had seen the German cultural references to Nordic rage, the German thunder of Teutonic war, and how Thor would destroy the Gothic cathedrals:

'Do not smile at my advice, the advice of a dreamer who warns you against Kantians, Fichteans, and philosophers of nature. Do not smile at the visionary who anticipates the same revolution in the realm of the visible that has already taken place in the realm of the spirit.'[1]

Heine saw Christianity as a bulwark against the Teutonic, warlike character. Cultural revolutions are like lightning strikes: they arrive quickly, without warning, and leave a wasteland of the values which went before. The foundations are torn up by the iconoclasts of the new movement, of excited youth. The French Revolution, the Russian Revolution, Mao's Cultural Revolution, and now, the liberal attempt to impose a selective virtue to existing norms through the unravelling of the family and the suffocating stamp of the State and technology into all walks of life. Heine had predicted this; he saw the destruction of the natural law and theological views of humanity. He foresaw the squashing of the human spirit, of human destiny. That thought precedes action, in the virtue-signalling US universities to its fawning servants in the media at CNN and the BBC, the Heine nightmare arrives like a thunderbolt. Truth requires that moral individuals stand up to historical aberrations by revaluing truth and fighting for a moral goodness. Truth is embedded in the past and future of a teleological continuum which is based on the virtues of a public and private moral world.

At the level of philosophy, there has been a mixed conception of truth. The 'Correspondence Theory' of truth has classical origins; it goes back to Aristotle's claim in his 'Metaphysics' that truth corresponds to the way the world is, that a proposition meets a fact. These facts are mind-independent. For Aquinas, it was the meeting of the intellect with reality. The 'Coherence Theory' of truth believes that truth propositions must conform to some kind of system or coherent whole. Truth only exists within a system. Idealists, such as Kant, see a coherence theory of truth because of their metaphysical position. Kant believed in a division between the 'Phenomenal World' and the 'Noumenal World' (which is unknowable). From the idealists' perspective, reality is something like a collection of beliefs rather than objective facts. Therefore, there is a plethora of thinking even about what actually truth 'is', so it is not something easily arrived at. Hence the dilemma in claiming the truth for any side of the argument. In essence, the differences are epistemological rather than ontological. That is, they are really searching for the same thing, by differing routes.

A proponent of the Coherence Theory may say the methodology of arriving at a Correspondence theory to be naive;

that a truth needs to correspond to a fact, too simple. But Coherence Theory suffers from shifts in scientific knowledge. Non-Euclidean geometry, to some extent, partially undermines the apparent tautological nature of geometry, which was the bedrock of the rationalist's claims that reason can provide knowledge: other geometries are possible, and also true and consistent. Humans are both weak and unique, and any knowledge 'discovered' – true or otherwise – is discovered by a human, individual mind. The nearest we may get to objective truth is intersubjective truth, where we come to an agreement within our own culture. That is why truths often do not cross cultures and we need to take off our *kulturbrille* and work on our own cultural truth (hence the myths of cultural concepts such as rights, globalisation, development, etc). So, our definition of truth may need to be more expansive than Plato, Descartes, and other philosophers claim. A Pragmatic Theory of truth may be nearer to the mark: that truth is the 'thing that works'; it is achieved through the knowledge and experience of 'which things have worked'. If some other set of ideas works better, then that is true. Science is represented by the pragmatic theory in the sense that, what once rested, for example, on Newtonian mechanics, will change. At one time these beliefs were set in stone, then toppled like statues. These theories then do not correspond to the facts. However, if scientific theory advanced to the stage of a complete physical theory of the universe, then the Pragmatist would become akin to the Correspondence theorist. Therefore, people who subscribe to various theories of truth (methodology) may agree in the essential singularity and ontology of the search for truth. However, it is not the modern version of truth, the truth of 'cultural revolutions' – a woke sensibility neither based on objective realities or facts. Truth, for modern liberalism, is not on the menu.

For Heidegger, even the definition is the failing; he states that the original Greek conception of the word *'alethia'* meant 'unconcealment' and not the modern meaning of being 'correct'. Heidegger's argument was one of authenticity, that truth is concealed by the inauthentic aspects of life, through technological progress, which increases and removes man from authentic being. Therefore, like Aristotle, truth involves a form of unconcealment, or moving towards a teleology of the individual and a social virtuous path.

Truth can also be a way of viewing the world. The pre-Enlightenment world saw everything as having a purpose. These were contained within a 'natural order' which also recognised a 'teleology' or purpose to its nature. Reason, in the classical conception, was the guiding part of this destiny; others being passions and spirit, for example. This reason linked the immortal mind with the divine order of the Universe. The Enlightenment attempted a rethink on the metaphysics of this previous spiritual approach to the world. The concept of nature was now detached from the human. With Newtonian physics you have the arrival of the world as a self-regulating entity; it was this ideological transformation which facilitated the autonomous individual of Adam Smith. From this it becomes clear that people and the world are machines. So, the Enlightenment passed down the ideological premise that man was atomised, machine like and, through Kant, could be good, law fearing citizens. The ideological background was set to describe man as Machiavellian and acquisitive- and from there institutions and market capitalism had a philosophical base. The mistake of Marxism was to think that the economic determinist base came first. There is always the need to justify regimes and economies through ideological foundations.

The idea of a teleological purpose, which had been taken up by the Christianity of the Medieval period, was rejected. Knowledge, for Descartes, through his famous 'Cogitans' ('I think therefore I am'), became solely that of reason. This meant the duality of subject-object; the subject, and therefore reason, became the centre of the world view. Although Hume put 'passions' back on the Enlightenment agenda, it was nullified by Kant in his sanctification of reason and the substantive world reason. Therefore, the mind is able to posit universal laws; through his 'Categorical Imperative', there is a universal law. Individuals can act as they wish as long as the objectives fit into a Universal Law, recognised and accepted by the community.

What Kant attempted was to construct a solution to metaphysical questions of the world, through reason. Therein, questions such as 'what is existence?', 'how should I live?', 'what is human nature?' were articulated through reason. In his *Critique of Pure Reason*[2] Kant put forward the notion that reason was the cornerstone of morality through 'transcendental logic', which was more than the formal logic of science, for example. However, the removal of metaphysical, religious, and aesthetic traditions has meant that, in the modern period, reason has become formalised. Reason has become delimited by the closing of the world of political discourse through legalistic restrictions on speech, and also media/social media bias. There has then been a diminution of ideas of spirit and particularly a moral trajectory, which is accentuated by reason being an essentially Occidental idea.

The fact that reason also posits a static notion of enquiry-fixed in the contemporary world (what is reason may morph from one epoch to the next) ignores notions of history, of tradition, what some philosophers have called 'disclosure'. In this, there is a whole aspect of background ontological worlds to see, rather than the formal reasoning of logic. Under the existing paradigm of reason, we are unable to disclose possibilities of another viewpoint. In pre-modern societies, the underlying unified vision of reason was able to answer the questions such as 'how we should live', but the modern world has formalised approaches to a narrow vision of administrative, bureaucratic or technological reason. Without the opening of the universe of reason to other paradigms, questions of fundamental significance about how we should behave, how we should structure societies, are imprisoned in an arbitrary fashion. To disclose truth and justice, the shackles of the Enlightenment need to be cast off and a type of unconcealment begun. In many ways, the truth debate boils down to the juxtaposition between Hobbesian and Rousseauian theories of man; are we nasty and brutish, or are we, devoid of civilisation, communal and caring? For if we adopt the Hobbesian view, we are chained to authoritative structures, on the one hand, to control human behaviour, or we can return to the original fecundity of a moral path as outlined by Aristotle. This path places humans in the Rousseau mode, and only corrupted by 'civilisation'.

The entire zeitgeist of the 80s, 90s was 'the selfish gene'. Richard Dawkins's *The Selfish Gene*[3] promised a Copernican revolution of thinking; it captured the minds of most scientists and, most importantly, captured the zeitgeist of the increasing 1970s' fetish for supply side-economics and monetarist thinking. There is no society, only individuals. It seemed to align with that age-old idea – promoted by Machiavelli, by the Enlightenment, by religions, by Hobbes – that man is selfish, and it fitted onto the era like an errant glove. Even in contemporary times you can still find academic articles banging the tin drum: 'Forty Years of The Selfish Gene Are Not Enough'[4].

The leitmotif of much of Dawkin's book centres around the concept that genes, not the organisms, are 'selfish', in that they replicate for themselves rather than the organism. Organisms are merely survival machines, and altruism is no more than the selfishness of genes. Before Dawkins, it was all about natural selection refining the behaviour of the living organism in order to promote the continuing of an individual, family, or species. Now, said Dawkins, it was the gene that was running the show, with us as merely robots and machines. The new zeitgeist was transformed from an essentially quirky scientific footnote, into mainstream media justification for the 'self'. However, it was part of the underlying premise of post-Enlightenment thought, of rationality, of the limits to charting a course of moral virtue. We are constrained, by genes, into accepting the desires and passions; constrained by the web of cultures built; constrained by governments and structures, unable to be 'part' of history. Now, genetic predisposition is joined with artificial intelligence, the science of media algorithms in moving free will away from the human and onto science. Genes, of course, show dispositions to certain illnesses, to autism, ADHD etc and can also dispose one to depressive conditions such as bipolar disorder and schizophrenia. There may be also therefore traits towards political affiliation, religion etc. However recent research into 'Epigenetics' has shown how the 'nature or nurture' problem is misconstrued. In this approach, 'tags' are placed on genes (from outside experience) and passed down through generations. For example, research into mice has shown how they search for the pleasant smell of cherries. However, when researchers combined this smell with a mild electric shock, it was revealed that a fearful memory of cherries was passed on to the children of these mice. The same traits were shown in descendants of US Civil War prisoners and Holocaust survivors who passed on trauma traits to future generations. However, 'Epigenetics' also has positive imprints such as tags for acquired new learning. This is illustrated with learning to ride a bicycle; increased exposure means the memory is increasingly accessed and this becomes habit, a default option. However, the negative aspect of Epigenetic transfer is that past traits become canonical; for example, beliefs, ideas. Consequently, nature and nurture are interrelated in a complex web although the ideas behind Epigenetics add further evidence to both innatism and nurture. As we have seen with Dawkinian genes, certain epochs can exaggerate one at the expense of the other and the default options of the brain can triumph the latest fad. On a cultural level, therefore, certain ideas can become *de rigeur*. What makes the present epoch disturbing is that these ideas are cemented by biased medias and corrupt elites. Free will is becoming increasingly delimited by technology and medias to the extent that innate ideas of community and ethics are clouded out.

The dominance of evolutionary scientism was seen in a type of secular deism. It was reinforced by the technological growth of societies. However, the Coronavirus spectacle has illustrated the contradictions within modernism. At once the slave to evolution and genes, secularism seems to offer up no transcendent quality to life. Evolution appears barbaric now: how could science do this? Now the 'selfish gene' is the 'heartless gene'. Whilst we have on one side a rationalistic view of death – the detached drone strike, easy abortions, euthanasia in Switzerland; but on the other, Covid-19 is unacceptable. What would have been tolerated by pre-Enlightenment societies as cyclical and inevitable is not tolerated by liberalism – there must be a way out. The convenient way out, the quintessential value of liberalism, was the lockdown. The established churches have shown moral cowardice in the face of this contradiction. Instead of juxtaposing the contradictions of liberalism, instead of condemning the State for the abuse of freedoms, of those with dementia, of cancer patients, it has shaken hands with liberal modes of thinking. The modern church is taken up, more and more, with the pyrrhic victories of appeasing secularism, and offers nothing transcendental to mankind's predicament. Liberalism entails the postponement of life; it means not being part of history, as history is increasingly the realm of elites, of technology. Man is now standing outside history, forced now to listen, to observe in virtual worlds, to wait for lockdown to work. Society has descended into liberal comfortism; there is no spirit, no fearlessness, no action. Man has delegated these things to an accumulative elite, and exchanged it for the bliss of modernity, technological stupor, and pharmaceutical happiness.

In various periods of history, there are attempts to rationalise the present, particularly if it is unpleasant, unfair, or has disastrous consequences. The current epoch of industrial organisation, which began in the mid-nineteenth century, was a seismic shift in the organisation of societies. The leitmotif was the replacement of traditional time with artificial time. It meant the displacing of humanity from agricultural modes of existence (agriculture itself having uplifted people from a previous existence of hunter-gatherer). Capitalism saw a radical shift in perceptions of time and space. Time was now regimented, and the introduction of the clock appeared alongside automation and factory production. Time was now something controlled from outside the human. Man had replaced the teleology of a prior existence into a rationalised one. It was no longer a cyclical time of seasons and fertility rites, of magic-controlling chiefs and sacrificial rites. Space had changed also. No longer was it the vast horizon of field to be farmed; man had been transplanted to the metropolis, to toil in that Lowry landscape, no longer an actor in a bright Breughel painting, vivid and mad. Now, in the technological revolution, space is the Munch-like figure in front of a computer screen, and nature is something reported on a plastic TV screen, on a National

Geographic channel. Space and time are now 'virtual'; the necessity of capital organisation requires homo sapiens to live in a virtual space world of internet banking and shopping, crouched over a plastic box. Time is still regimented, and the metropolis more and more blocks out any appreciation of independent sun-time; schools demand more and more time of their pupils; the workplace demands more hours, even weekends. In a nutshell, the conceptions of space and time have been disembedded from the traditional experience of man.

The question arises: has this disembedding been a result of a conscious process or an unconscious process? Is it really, as the likes of Francis Fukuyama[5], for example, would have us believe, the inevitable march of historical necessity, that liberal march of progress to the wonder world of liberal democracy? Or is it a conscious unravelling fostered by an accumulative cabal? Certain periods or epochs in history require intellectual justification, for they lack a consistent moral path. The divine right of kings – the idea that authority is given by God and cannot be removed except by God, was the justification made by the Church for monarchical regimes. 'Reason' was used as the justification for the blood-letting of Robespierre. When Bakhunin wrote, 'The urge to destroy is a constructive urge', he was swimming in a sea of conviction; the conviction that anything is justified as long as the long march is reached. Truth is something which only the usurper is privy to. From Machiavelli to Milton Friedman, there are people prepared to underwrite the notions of the regime, however unsavoury they may be.

However, recent research has shown that 'innateness' is back on the agenda after a few decades of obsessive attempts to prove the blank slate nurture hypothesis, that man is created by culture, whilst the reality is a symbiosis. The problem of modernity is that this innate tendency to groupness, to community, has been relegated by a progressive mantra. However, in all realms – from linguistics to morality – the sense of 'innate' ideas or forms is back in contention. 'Morality' or 'truth' was seen by Nietzsche as an ephemeral shifting iceberg of thought. However, *concepts were formed* in early human societies, although these concepts have been forgotten by modernity. The relics of Plato, of Aristotle, of Christianity, have become taboo. For most of humanity, homo sapiens were hunters and gatherers. It is only recently, very recently, that agriculture, the State has emerged. The Hobbesian description of the state of nature of all against all has become the accepted notion of civilisation. That man is a beastly thing which needs the Leviathan of the State to guide and control. The Rousseauian notion that man was essentially cooperative and decent had been replaced by the Hobbesian notion of selfishness and greed. It still pervades the media, the world of business, and it is so corrupting that it has flooded academia. Look in any discipline and you will find the Leviathan, the selfish gene. It underlies the notions of world governance, the EU; that paternalistic idea that the State knows best. However, the most disturbing aspect of this is not only that Hobbesian views are omnipresent; it is that they have been deliberately stoked and disseminated, despite the evidence. It is that science, academia, and government have prostituted themselves at the altar of reason, despite the evidence. What we are searching for is the truth. For to plan societies based on agendas, or selective choice, is something which we have done before – in Nazi Germany or in the Soviet Union. It is dysfunctional and does not work, for at its core it turns homo sapiens upside down and makes him behave like 'Homo Economicus'.

However, the real damage which such a reductionist approach does is to impute pure passivity into the population. It says, in effect, that we are blind automatons at the mercy of our genes. There is no point in trying to usurp it, to change yourself, to act ethically. It was, of course, a gift from the heavens for established elites. For this, combined with 'Homo Economicus', enabled monetarism to flourish. It underpinned the demonisation of equality modes of thought, of communal groups. So, we see in the 90s, and to the present, the diminution of groups and the elevation of the individual, but, more accurately, the 'isolation' of the individual – thrust into the market, and removed from family and community. Dawkins gave scientific respectability to destructive economic and social theory. He packaged this in a vitriolic attack on all forms of spirituality. Even before the publication of *The Selfish Gene,* modern biology had shown nature as a much more faceted entity than gene-driven. The new view sees nature as a complex of networked systems within an optimised system of evolution. Ecosystems are hugely dependent on the cooperation of entire species; cooperation has displaced individualism as new evidence emerges on why homo sapiens succeeded, through cooperation and language. The Coronavirus has shown how cooperative, homogenised societies fare better than disparate ones. The Cartesian world view of the Enlightenment, that nature is a machine, has been propagated in the modern era because the metaphor of the Enlightenment has become fact, with conceptions of the gene as 'code', and the mind is 'software' for the 'hardware' of the body. If the earth is a machine, then it becomes a lot easier to dehumanise it, which has led to the destruction of the environment and species on an unsustainable scale. Scientific Reductionism – the idea that everything can be reduced to the interaction of particles, of atoms, of genes – evolved from the extraction of science as a subject away from the unified days of the Philosophes, which incorporated both the humanities and science subjects. The autonomy of science was a result of the misunderstanding of reason; it was never meant to divorce from the philosophe. Modern complexity theory and research in systems biology have shown that both strands are being reunited, that it is the 'connections' between organisms that are more salient, not the entities themselves.

Whilst Dawkins is not advocating selfishness as the response of individuals to the invisible hand of the world, the writings emerge as a metaphor for behaviour. Once metaphors are proffered, and become engrained into popular media, they are difficult to get rid of. Dawkins writes:

'Be warned, that if you wish, as I do, to build a society towards a common good, you can expect little help from biological nature.'[6]

Dawkins presents to us the mind-body dualism of Descartes' Cogitans, going back to Plato's dualism between reason and the body. This thinking underscores the Christian metaphysic of the soul battling the body. However, although this is predominantly a Western duality, it does not reflect the findings of anthropology in other traditions, which show the essence of cooperation as part of human nature. It was a dangerous metaphor to peddle. Even though it had scientific validity at a micro-level, it ignored other aspects of evolution and has been discredited by new research into cooperation modes. For example, research into infant behaviour has shown innate modes of cooperation rather than conflict. In fact, new research overturns traditional ideas that babies are wild tyrants which need to be civilised by mothers and schooling. Paul Bloom and his colleagues looked at whether babies had a sense of naive morality. He notes the study of Joseph Henrich – a cross-cultural study which showed propensities of punishing unfairness in different cultures. The results showed that kindness to strangers and the punishment of unfairness was visible in large-scale communities:

'What do these findings about babies' moral notions tell us about adult morality? Some scholars think that the very existence of an innate moral sense has profound implications. In 1869, Alfred Russel Wallace, who along with Darwin discovered natural selection, wrote that certain human capacities — including "the higher moral faculties" — are richer than what you could expect from a product of biological evolution. He concluded that some sort of godly force must intervene to create these capacities.'[7]

It was Bloom's claim that most societies have some shared belief in notions such as fairness and kindness. This is where the human concept of empathy comes from – a sense of binding with our immediate group. Unfortunately, empathy's other side is fearfulness of strangers, and can lead to xenophobia. But for our kin, and immediate group, it makes sense within Natural Selection to behave like this at the gene level. This encourages the spread of kin selection; so, it isn't for 'selfish' reasons – it is for the survival of our 'group'. Further, it also means we cooperate with other groups. This meant that cooperation – for example, between hunter-gatherer communities – would have been based on the niceness rather than nastiness of other groups, as well as reciprocal benefits such as food, hunting, etc. This, therefore, would point to the innate nature of some moral concepts. Babies are known to be sympathetic to other babies crying; they appear to want to help people accomplish tasks (Warneken and Tomasello[8]). Perhaps this is more linked to compassion rather than morality. However, empathy was the guiding light behind most moral systems. The mistake, noted by Hume, was to place reason behind the Enlightenment conception of morality, when clearly our fundamental desires are neither rational or irrational. Therefore, there must be primordial innate concepts of goodness, which remains in the human makeup. To place only reason behind the world – the reason of the law, or science – results in the irrational nonsense of unfair judicial sentences, Hiroshima, the Holocaust, and the virtue of movements consumed by reason alone. Hume wrote:

'Tis not contrary to reason to prefer the destruction of the whole world to the scratching of my finger.'[9]

Take the recent case of a woman arrested during the Covid lockdown in the UK. She tried to take her mother away from a care home. According to special legal powers, the elderly inmate was a ward of court of the care home during the Covid crisis. In normal times, she would have been legally free to go wherever she pleased. As she suffered from Dementia, the daughter – a qualified nurse – wanted to remove her, but was barred by the care home. This was *de rigeur* for the law, but inadequately expressed the feelings behind the situation. It fails to accommodate ideas of equality and fairness; it is a tool often used by institutions to hide behind unpalatable practice. It is tantamount to the inability of judicial systems to find equitable redress, to the 'slave to the law' inhuman views of courts. In the new world of reason, the individual is a mere appendix to the law. As Mr Bumble opined in *Oliver Twist*, 'The law is an ass.'

Evolution can explain our kindness to our kin group; this is where the genetic factor works. Then how do we account for higher altruism, the acts of kindness to strangers? Those who fall on the pavement, or donating your blood to the blood bank? Many actions do not merely fulfil a utility function for our genes, or to further reproductive capacities. Ideas opposed to racism, our repulsion towards genocides, to animal cruelty, are innate reactions to the suffering of others. Babies' altruism is aimed at their own group, rather than in faraway places. The later, developed morality of adulthood is a cultural one, moulded onto and developed from the altruism of innate ideas. The infants' primordial sense of justice, of fairness – if even to the nearby group – influences the cultural mode, but we are in no way a 'blank slate' from birth. Of course, this idea of 'nearness of relations' was axiomatic to most communities in the Medieval period; the average citizen rarely travelled more than a fifty-kilometre radius away from home in a lifetime. Communities had little overlap, except in times of war or long- distance trade. Therefore, 'aversion' to the stranger, the unfamiliar, meant that conceptions of the 'group' and the 'community' were very strong. There was no concept of a 'multi-cultural community'; in fact, it would have been seen as dysfunctional. Concepts, likewise, such as abortion, would have had no sense to pre-Enlightenment man; they would have been regarded as something alien to the essence of man. Therefore, we need to draw a truth or ethical policy based on innate conceptions or forms, not on episodic fashions. Innate cultural notions of justice and impartiality became evolved into religious systems – Christianity, Buddhism, and Islam. The mistake was to impute reason as being a higher form than the ideas which came from the state of nature. Civilisation, as Rousseau noted, was in these respects a backward step, in that it allowed reason and technology to disembed the human from a community of spirit and cooperation.

Therefore, to make a decision based on reason is a fallacy. There are always preferences, desires, which come *a priori* before reason. This, and further through Kant's obsession with reason, has led to the irrationality of decision-making, from courts to environment to human rights; reason has replaced humaneness or innate ideas as the guiding force. This was the mistake of the Enlightenment, and the effects are witnessed throughout modernity with cataclysmic consequences. Therefore, whilst concepts such as morality and truth move with the flux of history's ebbing tide, there are moral constraints, innate ideas of goodness or forms, which we are given, which can't be replaced by reason without seeing the inhumanity of the present milieu and the disjoint behind the reason of the state and the nature of man. In essence, therefore, truth has been superseded by reason and our innate capacities falsified. Metaphors such as 'the selfish gene' over-cook the claims of genetic evolution and move away from truth, not nearer to it. In the post-World War 2 environment, there was a need to explain the horrors of war. How could the rational, cultured Germans do that? At the time, it was rational to see the viciousness of humans as a trait, a part of human nature which Hobbes had picked up on. Human beings were essentially bad – a fall from grace, the bad apple of the Garden of Eden, were the explanations. The zeitgeist of academia, of science, echoed these beliefs, offering reinforcement. In the basement of Yale University in 1961, Stanley Milgram had his volunteers (teachers) administer the famous electric shocks to a 'learner' in an adjacent room. Instructions to increase the shocks were continued until the levels were fatal (if they had been real). The 'shocking' results were that 65% of the teachers were prepared to give the last fatal shock when told to do so by the authority figure. The results were unexpected, but the general message was clear: human beings are obedient to authority despite their moral makeup. It was a pertinent reminder, around the time of the Eichmann trial, of how the Germans were 'obeying orders'.

In his book *Obedience to Authority: An Experimental View*, he maintained that the arguments against his experiments were fuelled by an unwillingness to accept the truth about human nature, in that it was debased and immoral. Milgram himself, before the start of the experiments, had believed that if the participants had been German, the results would have been even more stark. Therefore, all humans have the potential to obey authority, but some humans are more obedient than others. It discounted, no doubt, the British bombing of Dresden, and would have recoiled later from the mass bombing of Vietnam and Cambodia by American soldiers. However, besides the issue of whether aspects of human nature are general or specific to 'the Germans', the main point was offered: that human nature is rotten. It was a timely explanation for the Holocaust, or so Milgram thought. However, some recent interpretations of the experiment reveal interesting and fundamental misapplication of the experiments. Moti Nassani[10] argued that the 'obedience' was not obedience to evil but a preconceived notion in the goodness of scientific enquiry and institutional benevolence. That is why the individuals administered the shocks, not their natural deference to authority. We become accustomed to believing in the neutrality of institutional rationality: the BBC is independent and neutral, although the evidence is not so. The BBC is more and more biased to representing one set of political opinion – the liberal Weberian left. We have, through media embalming, through 'gaslighting', developed an unawareness of institutional and State theft – that is the complacent acceptance of public sector rhetoric which hides the real nature of these institutional monoliths. The ideological underpinning is that these institutions of science and State must produce good; the 'in the interests of science' perspective. Other social psychologists have argued that the desire to follow orders is less marked than the 'Experiment requires you to continue' type of prod. Again, it is the belief in scientific enquiry which underlies the Milgram experiment, not blind authority. Nevertheless, there is agreement amongst social psychologists that 'distance' from the learner (victim) facilitates the following of orders, and in many ways this echoes the nature of groupness and the aversion to the unfamiliar, which is part of the infants' innate makeup. So, whilst group affinity has its positive attributes of aiding our kin, it also has negative effects *vis a vis* xenophobia. The innate goodness of human nature is a two-sided coin. In every epoch, science will attempt to validate the prevailing sentiment of the governmental or societal outlook – what I term the 'Scientific Zeitgeist'. Milgram was no different to Dawkins in this respect.

The retort to ideas of a corrupted human nature goes back to Aristotle. Aristotle's view was that the human inclination to behave ethically is dependent on the good state, the *polis*. Admittedly, this was based on notions of the Homeric poems and the small Greek city state, and hence its lament in the modern period. That it is difficult to reconcile the rationalities of the social role with individual life would not have been lost on Aristotle. However, he would not have envisaged the sudden plunge into anomie which civilisation has undergone. It appears impossible to merge the two in contemporary circumstances; hence the flight to individualism. Some Islamic societies make a decent fist of it, but even those are open to the plague of globalisation, corrupt regimes and technologies. Ideas such as 'the selfish gene', globalisation theory, Homo Economicus, are ideological and media-driven constructs to enable the elite manipulation of resources.

This accumulation has resulted in the mass anomie we witness in contemporary societies. This anomie has resulted in a divided homo sapiens, driven by medias to believe in globalisation and consumerism, whilst at the same time moving the individual away from a sense of innate purposes and rooting. Technology and medias divide, not unite. Truth, in this sense, as corresponding to a deeper reality, has been hidden and usurped by technology and medias. Media and social media have replaced subjective thought and understanding with biases, and algorithmic decoupling of individuality from free will and choice, although the majority of individuals do not even know it. In the next two chapters, we examine the influence of these sectors. Rousseau had remarked that 'everywhere man is in chains'. It was self-evident; the prison of the factory and school 'panopticon', the trampling of factory labour, the iron fist of authority. Man is now unaware of the chains, swathed in technological blindness and pharmaceutical bliss. It could for some be a form of comfort; the comfort of repeated metaphors which become sacrosanct. Truth now is like coins which have lost their engravings, and are only metals. The contemporary ethos vindicates a morality of the 'good' and 'virtuous', played out in caricatures of liberal sentiments such as BLM and any other fashionable *cause celebre*. Virtue is now dependent on media whims. But this cowering to petty virtues hides the real. As Huxley mentioned, it is 'dictatorship without tears'. A comfortable soporific of consumerism and vacuous thinking, as liberties are removed painlessly and efficiently by technology and the State.

In the science fiction classic *A Canticle for Liebowitz*, by Walter M. Miller, a Catholic monk hides out in an old monastery after a nuclear war and tries to pick together the remnants of lost books, in order to salvage a vision from the wreckage of civilisation. The Tower of Babel moment could be the introduction of agriculture or the Enlightenment, or the Industrial Revolution. Or it could be the suffocation of freedom through the Technological turn. These moments demand restructuring the mess from the remaining rubble. Today's moral discourse is a distortion of the classical sense of *moralis* or *etikos* which imputed more the telos of 'character' enhancement. It was the Enlightenment project that encapsulated a modern view of morality, but it was based on concepts such as 'utility' and 'rationalism'. We have been left with the rubble of these precepts, which were conveniently embedded into liberal economic systems. Kant clung to reason with his 'categorical imperative'; Diderot turned to 'passions'; Hume to 'desire'. However, none of these came close to meeting the Aristotelian path. Aristotle was attempting to sketch a path of ethics whereby how we run our lives to achieve the human telos. *Both* the institutions of state and the behaviour of individuals had to be ethical. It was the Enlightenment which detached telos from existence and substituted reason. With that, Aristotle's requirement of ethical tutoring, to achieve the telos, was lost.

Therefore, modern claims to ethical statements are based on the arid assumptions of Enlightenment thought. Moral precepts have the ability to correct deviations from human nature, in the movement towards the telos. The Enlightenment wanted to impose a stand-alone ethical system without a telos, and here it failed; they failed to incorporate the tradition of the past. Modern ethical systems, be it Kant's Categorical Imperative or utility or human rights, fail precisely because they lack the telos of underlying guidance. They appear as empty ether in the modern wasteland. Therefore, the modern world replaces telos with petty protest, virtue signalling, rights watch fetishes. In modern parlance, human actions are explained, or excused, in a diaspora of social science research which takes a mechanistic view excluding telos. Individuals are reduced to Homo Economicus, atomised agents, selfish genes. Without moral teleology, we are left with efficiency, managerialism, and Weberian bureaucratic rationality. This bedevils all attempts at public policy, government, health care. We are now at the point of juncture of the Easter Islanders when they first met the European explorers – unable to explain the telos or meaning of the statues of the modern world.

The Engineer of Human Souls: How the Media Shapes Modern Man

When John Milton heard of the flogging of agitator John Lilburne, who had been imprisoned for importing seditious books, Milton wrote the world's first and greatest defence of free speech called the 'Areopagitica' in 1644. He said that 'he who destroys a good book, kills reason itself, kills the image of God, as it were in the eye'. He named the pamphlet on account of the hill Areopagus, overlooking Athens, where debates raged and justice was executed in the halcyon days of Greek democracy. It was a radical piece, in an England where printing presses were strictly controlled by government. In effect, Milton said that a wise society needs the ebb and flow of conflicting ideas, and that people must have open minds because 'truth' was not owned by anyone. A dark curtain has been drawn across the world. That is the curtain of prescriptive institutions. From traditional supporters of liberty, such as the free press, institutions, corporates, and even within the realms of entertainment, free speech and thought has become Dickensian. For in the world of the woke liberal, freedom is something which need not be debated. In the words of Marxist Herbert Marcuse in his infamous paper 'Repressive Tolerance':

'Liberating tolerance, then, would mean intolerance against movements from the Right and toleration of movements of the Left.'[1]

For Marcuse, it was capitalism and patriarchy that were the origins of inequalities, and the road forward was not one of educated debate but intolerance to others' opinions. From the seeds of the Frankfurt School has sprung its, rather less intellectual, prodigy: Identity Politics. For it was the increasing realisation of the likes of Horkheimer and Marcuse that the traditional working-class (which they had previously believed to be the harbingers of revolution) did not actually agree with the Ivory Tower *trahison de clercs*. The traditional working-class had aspirations for home ownership, cars, and TVs. They had the unforgiveable temerity to want those things which the middle classes took for granted. The global revolution had not materialised; there must be another way. The other way was to push the agendas of repressed 'minorities'. This encompassed feminism, gay rights, black power. From now on, some groups would take on special privileged status. The agenda is an attack on the foundations of free speech and pluralism, and a bigotry towards religiosity in any form. What is deeply disturbing about the rise of this contemporary movement, is its lack of any intellectual foundation. It is designed to undermine working-class people considered 'racist' and 'nativist'. The foot soldiers of Identity Politics are the unemployed remains of vacuous universities in the US and UK, hoping to find virtue in a divisive and corrupt movement. The movement has polarised opinion into camps; it is the antithesis of the radical movements of the sixties, for it lacks any sense of historical position, community, tolerance, or historical knowledge. Identity Politics establishes a position by opposing/denying the other. Feminists invoke 'ad hominem' Dworkian enemies. BLM stands as something against the other white privilege. All these movements share one thing; their parochial hatred of other. Whatever intellectual justifications they have are more akin to Stalin's 'Engineering of Human Souls' than any romantic revolution. The communal movements of the 60s, of liberation theology, of traditionalism seek to unify, to establish community, to build bridges of hope.

Critical Theory, in essence, was an assault on the vestiges of Western culture. This normative attack on culture was premised on demeaning the family, notions of sex, and thousands of years of religious belief. It attacked patriotism and nationalism and all forms of tradition. The problem with this normative philosophy was that it lacked any analysis of historical anthropology. Through rigid indoctrination in schools and universities, in the mainstream media, a constant narrative is thrown out which creates this brave new world. The democratising of the media has become a pertinent aspect of the modern epoch. Democratising means the ability of academics, institutions, and social scientists to pontificate on the broad stage of social media. Of course, the problem with social media is it does not get the benefit of editing, unlike a journal, etc. The death of expertise has meant the explosion of irresponsible and ignorant content which the public take as fact. Democratisation does not mean an ever-expanding horizon of quality. In fact, the quality is increasingly side-lined for political correctness institutionalised by a legalistic framework in favour of restricting free speech for 'correct democratisation'. The assertion of correctness over quality is not now reserved for the libberati at the *Guardian* or CNN, but in so-called respectable institutions.

The vapid fumes of correct thinking have spread their wings. Whilst researching this book, I came across a quote on the Internet: 'Ethnic minority pregnant and *birthing people* (my italics) suffer worse outcomes and experiences during and after pregnancy and childbirth.' Birthing people?! However, this was not from a Democrat think tank or the Department of Gender Studies at Berkeley. It was from Harvard, the flag-flying American university renowned for scholarly business innovation. In the US, using the wrong pronoun could become a hate speech violation. The traditional, accepted nuance of using 'he' to describe wider humanity is facing criticism from correct people. Gender-free pronouns are all the rage for new liberal sentiment, even if they defy the logic of grammar. Large swathes of the public simply do not trust output now from any public institution or university – so removed from reality are many of these academics within the social sciences. This has led to a distrust of institutional integrity and quality. The media, in recent years, has abandoned truth. There has been an attempt to inculcate a system of guilt over slavery, black repression, etc. This has been highlighted by the extrapolation in the media of certain events, such as the death of George Floyd and police brutality, in order to force the agenda on the public. Certainly, there have been many cases of police aggression in the US – not all directed towards black people, but the conclusion is one of institutional racism. The Coronavirus and George Floyd events have given the liberal left a revolutionary opportunity to push through their Trojan horse of intolerance and anti-freedom, but it isn't a new strategy. Journalism today largely consists of 'opinion forming'. Whatever the extent of the so-called investigative journalism of the past, made famous in films such as *All the President's Men*, it has long since vanished, except, perhaps, for the intellectual vigour in the *National Review*. When Timothy Crouse wrote: 'It occurred to me that the networks regarded themselves as omnipotent and sacred institutions, roughly like the Presidency', he was writing 50 years ago. Imagine what he would have thought about today's opinionated, politically correct diatribes? The new liberal media of CNN and the BBC lack any of the ethical pretentions of their forebears. This affront to truth has infected not just journalism, but the entire cultural output, from Netflix to Hollywood to theatre, and to the good old Booker Prize. Stalin's maxim about writers and artists being the 'The Engineer of Human Souls' has never been so perfectly executed. Only now, there isn't the intellectual vigour – merely an overdose of wokeful mendacity. When Shelley said that poets were the 'legislators of the world', he did not mean for the bookless woke generation to take this literally. The writing of history has become flowery and vapid. All of American history is to be viewed through the lens of slavery, according to the 1619 project. Real history employs the facts and allows its readers to judge them critically. AJP Taylor, Gibbon, Ashbridge, Hugh Thomas, do not bombard you with comments such as the 'Aztecs were racists' or 'Shakespeare was anti-Semitic' on page one of their *billet-doux*. The raging woke warrior berates the reader with 'Queer Theory', 'Institutional Racism', 'Intersectionality', 'Critical Race Theory', with faux attempts at intelligence. Modernity has inflicted the curse of the mobile Munch phone to displace bookish thought, and the result is nothing to rival the likes of TS Eliot, Robert Frost, Hemingway, or Camus. Technology is displacing quality. Is it any wonder that Kurt Vonnegut despised the internet, or Ray Bradbury refused to acknowledge the automobile revolution? Yet they both write about future days.

In his *Bradbury Speaks* (2005), a collection of non-fiction essays, Bradbury argues for a break, a mass unplugging from technology, a time to reflect. In the story 'The Pedestrian', Bradbury imagines a dystopian future where the protagonist takes a walk and is subjected to an interrogation by law enforcement. If only it were fiction. The book forecasts a world where technology produces unnatural addictions. In 'Fahrenheit 451' firefighters are summoned, not to extinguish fires but to burn books. He predicts cancel culture by saying the burning of books was the result of pursuing hopeless utopian ideas. Whilst the 1950s were known as the 'Age of Criticism' in literature, with Edmund Wilson and Iris Murdoch, we now have 'The Age of Conformity' – the result being a public losing faith in media and the arts. Yet real truths can only be found in literature and poetry; they transcend the fad and the fashionable, even the epoch. They get to the root of the human spirit. That is why dictators are quick to silence the transcendent beauty of true artists. Truths often conflict with ideas; the great novels question conformity, seek to offer the reader another world, another culture. Literature is to travel down the Congo River to the *Heart of Darkness*. Its purpose is to meet Colonel Kurtz, not Kamala Harris.

The Madness of Reason

We are now standing at a 'liminal' flux in the present historical period. Beliefs are up in the air, on hold, uncertain. The transient ideas of modernity – Reason, Capitalism, Communism – are at a crossroads of uncertainty. The post-Enlightenment celebration of all things material and empiricist now seems redundant. The replacement of morality and ethics by a deliberate materialism has produced a divided homo sapiens, unsure of their footing in a rootless, ungrounded world. The question concerning 'how should we live?' has occupied the thoughts of the early Greek philosophers and the exponents of the Axial age religions, who placed their ideas of truth, morality, and ethics in a belief in some divine origin or myth. Here, truth is not something 'correct', but the truth of the real essence of man.

The Axial age produced a plethora of syncretic thinking in different parts of the world, from Moses handing out the Ten Commandments on Mount Sinai, to the Zarathustrians debating the flames of good and evil in Persia. In the 5th century BC the Buddha floated the idea of 'Sramana' or asceticism; ideas of karma. Plato's ideas of divine forms laid the basis of the Platonism which would later influence Christianity. These ideas all had a common thread – that of a divinely-inspired morality or ethics. It was not to humans to seek answers to metaphysical questions, but to the gods. It could be argued that the Enlightenment was another Axial moment in history; an amelioration of scientific thinking in an increasingly materialistic age. However, the assumptions of post-Enlightenment thinking have embodied an historicist account; some 'progress', a dialectic working towards the end of history. Perhaps this Axial age is unfinished, perhaps the world is indeed working to the scientific and technological apogee of humanity. However, the evidence does not support this view. Something is clearly wrong about recent modernity, something dysfunctional. Statistics on drug abuse, homelessness, the effects of globalisation, rates of depression, existential threats, in contemporary 'developed' societies, would suggest the way of the world is perhaps not linear, but cyclical, and that the Axial age of the Enlightenment is coming to an end.

It comes as no coincidence that the era of the Axial religions came at a time of the introduction of coinage and extended commerce throughout the world. The anthropologist David Graeber[1] notes that the development of coinage in three epicentres reflected the rise of the new philosophy centres. The rise of commerce, one which came out of a movement into agriculture and state-based entities, provided the division of society into commerce and religion. The surplus value of these societies enabled an elite class of thinkers to emerge, to make sense of the things around them – famines, wars, and disease. The three regions of Axial awareness were China, the Middle East (Occident), and India: there were similar ideas revolving from the Confucianism of the Chinese to the Buddhism of India, the Zoroastrianism of Persia, and in the West, the rise of Platonism. As trade increased, these societies were able to afford a kind of Troubadour priest, who, also aligned to commerce, began paving the road of the latter Silk Routes, exchanging ideas in dimly lit proto caravanserais. In this way, esoteric ideas touched other modes of thought, and the resulting stew was a spicy mix of the other. At the start of the Axial periods, therefore – like any new zeitgeist – you see the exciting yearning for knowledge and truth. Then, the troubadours are replaced by the administrators and they stagnate into organised religions, forgetting the myth and dynamism that created them. They become corrupted, and into this cyclical dialectic you get the Enlightenment – another attempt to revalue knowledge and truth. The Enlightenment exemplified reason and science, and ridiculed spirituality, ancient forms. Kantian reason replaced notions of innate primordial ideas. The problem with most eras of Axial thinking is that they become canonical. This can be forgiven in the sense that concepts are really, as Nietzsche pointed out, metaphors invented by humans to facilitate communication. But they become embodied in ways of thinking, solidified in thought. The Enlightenment canonised reason; the modern world has incorporated reason into the apparatus of a technological faith.

The underlying assumptions of science, of economics, is that man is rational. This means that man makes rational choices; it is the 'rational agent theory' of economics. This was driven by the Enlightenment belief in reason, and later reflected in the theories of the likes of Bentham, and utilitarianism; the greatest happiness of the greatest number could be arrived upon by scientific deduction and rational planning. The man on the Clapham omnibus believes that he is making informed, rational choices – his choice of supermarket food, the insurance he buys, the car. However, what if we were to speculate that not only are these domestic choices highly suspect, but they are manipulated by technology and algorithms, by Google, by tech giants? This pervasive influence can also be extrapolated to 'external' political choices such as voting, conceptions of authority, other cultures, and other religions, etc. Authentic choice has been obscured in a veil of distorted language and framing.

Consider the statements describing the outcome of a football match: 'Team A won'; 'Team B lost'. According to philosophers, you would say that they are equivalent; they say that their 'truth conditions' are equivalent. If one of these statements is true, then it stands that the other is true. For economists also, they would ascertain that they are the same in meaning. However, although logically equivalent, the associations of both statements have different meanings to different people. For some, there will be the association of incidents during the game – a penalty disputed, a dive in the box, the biased referee. Therefore, supposedly logical equivalent statements have alternative ideas of truth for different people. The conclusion would have to be that human beings cannot be counted on to be rational agents. There is far more going on in the world of the human than reason. Take, for example, the Covid pandemic. Public policy approaches within various countries followed an 'ad hoc' approach, some following scientific advice, others with public pressure glancing over their shoulder. Let's say there are two options[2] for the pandemic in a country which is predicted to kill 600,000 people:

Policy A means 200,000 will be saved.

Policy B means there is a one-third possibility that 600,000 people will be saved, and a two-thirds possibility that no-one will be saved.

It has been shown in psychology experiments that the majority of the public, if given the choice, will choose the first option. It is the certainty over the gamble.

In a second variant:

Policy A means 400,000 will die.

Policy B means one-third possibility that nobody will die, and a two-third possibility that 600,000 will die.

However, in the second variant, the majority chose the gamble version, although the outcomes in Version 1 and Version 2 are identical. People chose the supposed 'good' outcome. It was not a rational choice.

In the United States, this exact same experiment was given to public health officials concerned with decisions regarding vaccine allocation, etc. These professionals were tricked by the same gullible framing techniques as members of the public, with the same results. The frightening conclusion of framing techniques within psychology is that they are actively used in areas such as advertising, media, and social media, to deliver certain behaviour patterns which gazumps ideas of the autonomous free individual of liberalism. It becomes even more worrying when we ascertain that the same ideas are directing government and institutions, normally perceived as 'neutral'. Political parties can frame the issues on important decisions such as Brexit. Institutions such as the EU frame their public policy in benevolent, neutral language which conceals the real meaning behind the EU *raison d'etre*.

The Enlightenment developed the idea of the moral law; so, Kant's Categorical Imperative required such a construction of universality that the moral law applied to everyone. Rational agents are obliged to follow this moral law, although they are rational free agents. It is from their sense of moral duty and common good that they behave ethically, rationally. However, because homo sapiens are not rational (they have instincts, desires), there is a need for an objective, rational legal system. The Kantian system, therefore placed homo sapiens in a conflict between reason and desire. Schopenhauer believed a universal moral law unattainable and prescriptive; morality should be a system to guide human behaviour rather than an unreachable universal law. Nietzsche criticised Kant for adopting a normative system of metaphysics and ethics, and disputed the notion that morality could be found through reason. For Nietzsche, reason was merely one part of drives and instincts prevalent within man. Kant's universal self and autonomous will presumes that this autonomy of rational thinking extends to all men, independent of custom, tradition, and place. It presumes a very European conception of morality. Consequently, the edifice of the rational autonomous agent has had an undue influence on modern legislative and ethical formulations. Kant is right in believing in a set of *a priori* moral principles, although to ground these in reason is to place human nature in a strait jacket of his own tailoring.

Institutions do not make 'rational' choices precisely because of existing biases, elite manipulation, medias, and other influencing factors. The rational agent behind the invisible hand of the market does not produce good outcomes, as *prior heuristics* and *inherent biases* produce bad results. The idea of the Kantian autonomous individual will is in a desert created by the Enlightenment. Homo Economicus dominates public discourse; the individual, by pursuing self-interest, achieves public good. However, within any system, individuals will pursue more than material interest. Modern rational agent theory supposes that wants and desires be calculated and then policy implemented to satisfy them. It is the utilitarian approach. However, this makes a huge assumption that these desires *should* be satisfied. Public Policy should have a moral telos, a guidance narrative.

Even Marxists such as Jon Elster have attempted to broaden the rational agent model. Individuals, in game theory, make choices on expected benefits, but also judge the choices of others. The prevailing game theory view was that governments, for example, need to satisfy the preferences of all agents (this was the view of Utilitarian or Rational Choice theory). Elster, however, maintains that these agents themselves are consisting of an indefinite number of intertemporal agents with conflictions. This contrasts with economists' views that agents make descriptive choices. Elster says that economics cannot help but make 'prescriptive' normative judgements. Desires are also unreliable in the sense of being conditioned by previous history, by being conditioned by 'availability heuristics' (what is in the zeitgeist of the day, in the media, in culture) of the present or recent. Elster talks of 'adaptive preferences', whereby a person may prefer what he can have over what he can't have. This is due to the available choices. This is a psychological explanation for the durability of capitalism and its institutions. Take the case of a slave. If the slave owners and slaves are happy, they have adapted their preferences. That is ok with economic theory, because it is straight jacketed by descriptive analysis. If you were to use an evaluative approach, then you could not defend slavery as an institution. Elster says:

'We should not take wants as given, but inquire into their rationality or autonomy. These, in the general case, are properties that cannot be immediately read off the wants themselves... Rationality in the broad sense depends on the way in which the states are actually formed. Two individuals may be exactly alike in their beliefs and wants, and yet we might assess them differently from the point of view of rationality, judgment and autonomy.'[3]

Adaptive preferences have now been seen to undermine the autonomous agent, through medias and social media, algorithms. For example, rational choice might presume that we all want free speech. However, adaptive preferences have altered the Greek conception of 'parrhesia' so much that the present European conception would appear highly restrictive to the sophists. Therefore, we cannot 'assume' rational wants; we cannot allow paternalistic government to prescribe wants and needs. Modern liberalism works by pressing the limits of tolerance, to liberties and economies. People are forced to adapt their preferences akin to the gaslighting of the world. Consequently, to base public policy or a moral teleology on reason is akin to the constant adaptation – the fox who cannot reach the grapes will never reach the grapes because access to the vineyard of capitalism needs constant reinventing for the consumer; a constant adapting of preferences. The 'essence' of liberalism will never satisfy a true teleology; people are left with a constant feeling of 'sour grapes'.

The sunset of reason, ironically, was predicted by the Marxists of the Frankfurt School, Max Horkheimer and Theodor Adorno. In *Dialectic of Enlightenment*[4] they ask whether the reason of the Enlightenment – scientism – has become itself a salvation myth. Therefore, there is a dialectical process at work by which a movement contains the seeds of its opposite. The Enlightenment, rooted in individual autonomy, creates modes and systems in the economic sphere which enslaves future generations. The freedom becomes unfreedom. Science will be the solution to all problems. Horkheimer and Adorno, writing in 1944, saw the switch to scientism in the rise of fascism. However, that fascism was such a fleeting thing, it could not have been the real manifestation of the dialectic. In fact, fascism, from the philosophy of Julius Evola to Rene Guenon, was the opposite of Enlightenment thought; it drew inspiration from pre-Enlightenment thinking and metaphysics. What the dialectic was, in fact, was liberal democracy and its scientific rationalism. For Kant's Categorical Imperative of moral law has become the rigid, intolerant systems, laws, cameras, and dependency systems of modernity. The humanism of the Enlightenment has descended into a parody of 1984, with reason being the jailer of mankind; the jailer in the guise of the bureaucrat, the policeman, and the 'correctness' of those who are privy to 'making' history. The Covid days will be seen as an illustration of the illiberal tendencies of reason and modernity, how in the blinking of an eye the State can switch off existence without remit to the supposed cornerstones of liberalism – democracy and liberty. This is not an evaluative question as to whether the switching off is right or wrong on health grounds (most of us would agree). It unconceals the imprisonment of individuals in a rational system. Each epoch contains what Gadamer called a 'prejudice against prejudice'. But here the term 'prejudice' is neutral; it is a set of traditions and beliefs which guide our formulation of the present. These 'prejudices' are as much a source of knowledge as Enlightenment science. Subjects cannot, therefore, free themselves from the traditional past; notions such as rights and autonomy are phantom concepts of language without the background of formative history.

And now, in a dialectic on a dialectic, the tolerance-seeking liberals of the new Frankfurt School become the jailers of thought, as their criticism of capitalism and 'white privilege', in the moment of Democrat triumph, morphs into vicious intolerance and cancel culture. They themselves have become the jailers of Plato's cave, the ones now walking around with the keys.

The End of Globalisation and the New Westphalian System

They say if you stand in Times Square for twenty minutes, you will probably meet an acquaintance. In 1929, when Frigyes Karinthy wrote his 'Theory of Six Degrees of Separation', he stated that two anonymous individuals will be connected down the line through a sequence of six individuals. In recent years, global internet connectedness between individuals and communications have skyrocketed. We saw increased business cooperation, a depth of social organisations, flag-bearers of global governance (WTO, WHO, NAFTA, ASEAN, etc). However, a process of deglobalisation will be exacerbated by the Coronavirus shock and the incompatibility of elite government and people. The risk of increased interconnectedness has come with a price; a system with extensive interdependencies can be vulnerable to overload or external shock. This impact on a system can be seen in the scientific world of mechanics. Increasing loads can exacerbate the potential effects of shocks. Chaos theory shows how complex systems can be brought down by small variations across its spectrum – for example, forest wildfires and earthquakes.

Scientists call this the 'science of complex systems'. They essentially postulate three types of systems. A 'centralised' one, in which the entire network connects to a single central node. In politics, this could be seen, for example, in very centralised states. The second, 'decentralised' systems have separate hubs which are connected to the centre, but independent. This could be likened to a federalist structure of governance, for example. The third type, 'distributed' structure, is one in which nodes are all interconnected without a central position. Although we may have increasing connections and complex economies, increased connections can lead to collapse of systems. For example, the centralised Soviet Union tended to increase corruption and reduce efficiency at the periphery, as control and planning was centrally developed and ignorant to the people and market forces. Also, in 'decentralised' systems the individual nodes can become stressed by growing interconnectedness. This was visible within the EU, where financial bailouts of Greece between 2010 and 2015 amounted to about $400 billion, despite the fact that Greece accounted for less than 2% of European GDP.

Therefore, whilst growing interconnectedness on a technological sphere appears positive, the ramifications for more interconnectedness can be catastrophic. This has led to the collapse of globalised consensual politics and a resurgence of nationalist mantras in Europe and protectionist policies in the US. The problem with globalising systems is that they are always at the mercy of hegemonous powers; hence you see the corrupting influence of the US post World War 2: forcing economic liberalisation on culturally diverse countries. This is accompanied in globalisation by the 'export' of liberal culture; sexual and identity politics, unaccountable citizenship, attacks on 'nationalism' and 'patriotism'. The scale of the Coronavirus impact will, however, decouple the globalisation locomotive from the tracks, and will see a plethora of regional nodes adopting more centralised and nationalist procedures in order to protect their political economies.

The previous chapters saw how the late stage of neo-liberal capitalism is reaching its apogee due to the inherent contradictions of low growth, increasing inequalities, and the divorce of elites, through speculative accumulation, from the traditional productive nature of capitalism. The 1990s saw a plethora of journalists and academics proclaiming the end of history (again) narrative, and of globalisation being a conduit for social good and the alignment of global governance. Some historians, such as Peter Frankopan, in *The New Silk Road* spoke of a new Silk Road moving from the east, across the stans, through the caravanserais of the Islamic world and into Europe. However, this veneer of global homogeneity has been debunked by the new realities of growing nation statism and the Coronavirus shock, which effectively signals the sunset of a theory of globalisation. Complex problems of global governance, the spectre of League of Nations-type indolence in organisations such as the UN, the EU and NATO, have reduced globalisation to an economic trade system. That integrated political-economic governance system itself has fallen into disrepute with the realisation that the interests of global capital have taken a seat at the table of worldwide social governance. That the entire field of globalisation theory was more appearance than reality, and suffered from the same fate of 'end of history' narratives which have humbled the likes of Marx and Hegel. There has been a paradigm shift in the social sciences whereby various disciplines have been aligned to globalisation, but prematurely. It was understandable; the increasing interconnectedness of the world through the Internet and technology seemed to usher in a brave new world of political and economic governance. Theorists of globalisation argued that the new phenomena represented a change in historic assumptions about space and time. Anthony Giddens was one of the forerunners in taking up the case for globalisation as a transformative power, arguing that the quintessential difference of humanity now – compared to society in the pre-internet world – has been the discoupling of humanity from space and time. Giddens sees this in the sense that traditional man was 'in' space; it was limited by the physical surroundings or place. Time was perceived by the experience, as man moved around his environment. Now, with technology and globalisation, man 'appears' to have transcended time and space. Man can experience these things in virtual worlds – through the internet, television, and the media. Giddens sees this as a positive step; an alternative view to the concept of technology held by Heidegger, in that this disassociation from *authentic* space and time produces the alienation of man and a sense of homesickness from community.

What we have seen over the last few years is a retreat to Westphalia. It is, in essence, a realisation that cultural homogeneity on a worldwide scale is unrealistic. It is a realising that the nation state, whilst allowing elements of global capital to penetrate individual nation states, is far from redundant. In fact, we are now moving to a Westphalian realisation of the primacy of nationhood. The Peace of Westphalia in 1648 heralded in a legalistic assertion of nation state sovereignty and an end to the Thirty Years War; it was a response to the supra state philosophy of the Holy Roman Empire. It was a guiding principle of non-interference in other states. Nationalist tendencies in the nineteenth century evolved into the halcyon days of nation state formation, the search for identity. Consequently, attempts at global governance, such as the EU, are in effect affronts to the notion of state sovereignty. Their *raison d'etre* was always the economic hegemony of powerful nation states within that alliance (i.e. France and Germany). Although the Westphalian system was analogous to Europe rather than the 'Orient', it has become more relevant due to the emergence of peripheral nations, following the demise of colonisation in the twentieth century. It is, in many ways, a clutching back of democracy and culture from a cultural revolution attempting to impose undemocratic norms. This can be seen in the unaccountability of corporate giants and cultural organisations, NGOs, etc. Regardless of the veneer of international law, many states such as the US and China have unilaterally broken the consensus of the Westphalian system, by interfering in the politics of peripheral nations. Accounts of a post-Westphalian system of global governance, by the likes of Tony Blair, have been roundly discredited.

The Holy Roman Empire was transformed at Westphalia from a supra nation empire to a conglomeration of (albeit limited) independent 300 German principalities. The doctrine of *'cuius regio, eius reliogio'* (the religion of the Prince is the religion of the State) defined the cultural and political realms of a descaled entity. A return to Westphalian principles has been seen by many commentators as a means to return power to local constructs, of restricting the cultural leviathan of globalisation. Political scientist Stephen Walt in the US has urged America to embrace a new Westphalian system. Multi-national corporations exploit the fluidity and irresponsibility of a globalised marketplace by, for example, moving operations away in the light of increased corporate taxation, leading to unstable entities around the world. Despite the pronouncements about globalisation leading to the democratisation of world organisations and international relations, the reality has been very different. There is now a unilateralism and assertion by nation states which was seen at the time of the Iraq Wars and the Russian mission in the Ukraine. This is despite the fact that Globalisation Theory posited the end of the ideological and military divisions since the demise of the Soviet system. The theory was of epic proportions, and announced the global transformation of social relations in a new world. Michael Mann, in looking at the claims of social scientists, noted that:

'The human sciences seem full of enthusiasts claiming that a new form of human society is emerging.'[1]

The analysis of the period of the 1990s was that statist and national entities would be usurped by transnational forces of economics, technology, and social factors. It was a kind of 'post-Westphalian' system, dumping the nation state into the waste bin of history. However, whilst the appearance of a progressive globalisation seemed epochal, it was in essence only a fleeting temporal sense of change; it was merely a legalistic template formulated by international law, by bureaucrats who could do with reading Machiavelli or Nietzsche. Whilst 'liberation' seemed to be the catchword of the 60s, globalisation has reflected the zeitgeist of the 90s. Globalisation became a fashion, but an ephemeral thing. What we have seen, and no doubt will see, is a consolidation of political sovereignty in nation states. The march of history will show the collapse of the European EU enterprise and an increasing erroneous amelioration of capital into governance bodies, largely at a national state level.

The inherent limitations of global institutions can be seen in the theory of 'Structuration' (Anthony Giddens). Structuration works in a dialectic between a structure and systems. People manufacture society, although they are also limited by its rules. For example, language is a structure which has a generative set of rules called syntax. However, these rules also allow an infinite combination of words for new sentences. Therefore, structures such as religion, institutions, etc – although essentially stable – are modified and enhanced by human agency. In this sense, global capitalism exhibits some attributes of a system, but is not a globalised structure. There are limits to governance and the legal framework, the limits imposed by national sovereignty. The test of a structure would be how it responds to external shocks – for example, like the Coronavirus. In that sense, as we see with the impotence of the WHO, globalisation is weak. In times of momentous upheaval, shocks can bring down unstable or limited structures (as we saw with systemic collapse in traditional societies such as the Aztecs, etc). This has been highlighted in times of existential threat, pandemics, and war; systems are only as strong as the border of the nation state. The last few years has, therefore, started a process of de-globalisation. This reflects changes at a nation state level, as nation states assert themselves individually whilst disenfranchised groups (the urban working-class, minorities) become disillusioned with the ideology of neo-liberal capitalism. There has also been, quite recently, an awareness from the US of the growing size of the Chinese trade surplus and the colonisation, through takeovers and acquisitions, of strategic overseas companies. The rebuttal from the US has seen an attempt to decouple the Chinese locomotive from the tracks. The onset of the Coronavirus shock will further emasculate the globalised world as corporations seek to limit the consequences of external shocks by realigning supply to domestic or local markets. FDI (Foreign Direct Investment) shows a more pronounced decline weighted by GDP, and a steep decline after the financial crisis of 2008.[2] (see Appendix). This illustrates a trend of de-globalisation. The problem with liberal theories of globalisation was that they were naive about power bases within nation states and *de jure* legal limitations to international trade. For globalised world systems to operate effectively, they need the cooperation of states for this goal. The problem now is that there is domestic political opposition to globalisation in some 'populist' (traditionalist) and protectionist countries. The Brexit crisis revealed the weaknesses of the globalisation model, as the British decoupled from the economic bloc – seeing their own interests as paramount. This, however, also reflected the inherent contradictions of the EU, which gives greater influence to dominant states such as France and Germany. The liberal model of globalisation also relied upon the assumption that international organisations facilitate and regulate the process of global trade fairly. The model here is vulnerable to a conflict of interest among member states – for example, within the WTO. Here we saw in the context of the 'Doha Round' of the negotiations a divergence of interest between states wanting free trade and those seeing 'fair trade' as the leitmotif. Reneging on the brief can include establishing non-tariff barriers which can be reciprocated by other states. In a 2017 OECD survey, they found a steep decline in public support for globalisation which stood at only 53%, and a large minority which questioned immigration. Therefore, political changes in nation states are increasingly departing from the globalised message. The ideology of globalised markets has been sorely tested by the 2008 financial crisis and also the problem of the refugee crisis in Europe, with the perception that the EU was ineffective in solving the problem. The EU has been slow out of the blocks in organising the Covid vaccine for member states – indicative of a top-heavy, bureaucratic monolith unable to react to crises. Nevertheless, the left also criticise globalisation for its emphasis on neo-liberal corporatist and investment-centred structures, which unduly impact low-income groups and the environment. Globalisation in this sense also reduces pluralism amongst economic actors at home, as some are winners, some are losers – i.e. traditionally protected industries. This has been an increasing factor as Chinese goods destroy job markets in the US and worldwide. There has been a recognition that allowing imports to replace domestic production can have negative consequences for sectors deemed pertinent to national interests, such as the defence sector. Some critics of globalisation theory see it merely as a phenomenon of hegemony; that is, hegemonic countries are the ones that define policy and enjoy the lion's share of benefits. In times of hegemonic decline or external shock, countries can implement decoupling from globalisation. This was seen in the eclipse of Great Britain as a hegemonic power post-World War 2. The British Empire, a form of globalised market, saw its hegemonic empire contract and be replaced by other superpowers. In the contemporary milieu, there is the relative decline of the US as a major power. US GDP figures from the World Bank in 2018 show a relative steep decline in comparison to the rest of the world, and the figures are approaching equilibrium. The same scenario can be seen for defence spending – a relative decline as Chinese military spending rapidly catches up.

The Coronavirus impact will see the erosion of the globalised consensus which dominated the 1990s, and a move to regional trade agreements such as the Eurasian Economic Union of Russia, Kazakhstan, and Belarus. The new wealth of the region is reflected by these new developments. Hence, we will see a realignment of interests – one in which the US and Great Britain forge an economic pact, China sees its global acquisitions placed under further scrutiny by legalistic means, and the Russian alliance in the middle kingdom of the Stans forces its wealth into greater influence. Although the 'Lord of the Rings' may seem a far-fetched metaphor for world hegemonies, if you had forecast a world pandemic emerging in 2020 that would freeze the entire world economy, you would have been regarded with mock cynicism or, worse, recommended for psychiatric help. Who takes the position of 'Mordor' may only be a question of 'Kulturbrille' or Culture Glasses. It is likely that the rise of China will indeed be viewed through these lenses, and although its pathway may be stymied by lower economic growth and a contraction of globalised commerce, the political and military rise of China will set the agenda for world politics for decades to come. However, although many scholars have outlined the meteoric, inevitable rise of China – for example, Martin Jacques – many of their motives are less than ideological. Jacques is one of the now many UK apologists for China. There is now a large array of Chinese influence in the higher echelons of Western government and institutions. In *Hidden Hand: Exposing how the Chinese Communist Party is Reshaping the World* (Clive Hamilton, Mareike Ohlberg),[3] they show how the Chinese have infiltrated large swathes of Western institutions. For example, the book alleges that the London '48 Group Club', ostensibly an organisation to foster UK-Chinese trade relations, is active in grooming British elites in the ways of the CPP. The book maintains that the UK is heavily saturated with

Chinese influence. The object of such infiltration is to prop up legitimacy at home; if the British elites can be paid into banging the CPP drum, they must be respectable to people at home. Under an umbrella organisation called the 'United Front Work Department', a myriad of supposedly 'people to people' initiatives operate, whereby Chinese officials seek to influence Western diplomats and governments.

NSS (National Security Strategy) in the US has moved on from Obama's naive rhetoric about China, and its belief that incorporating China into world economic systems would lead to liberalisation in China. It was the perceived belief within political economy that political revolution follows economic liberalisation. The Chinese do not appear to be listening to the rhetoric of *The Guardian*, however. China's global outreach, through military threats and economic pressure, is the main conduit of China's export of a civilisational threat. The second Cold War is underway, whilst Russian hegemony is undermined by economic woes. The US and China, however, have economic reciprocity, whilst the first Cold War with the Soviet Union was ideological. China is playing catch-up in technology, quantum computing and, unfortunately for everyone else, vaccines. China has overtaken the West in banking technologies and the digital currencies of central banks. The Chinese are at the stage of pre-Colonial assertion, dominating supply chains, acquiring economic assets abroad, and buying off US and European elites. What has been called the 'Thucydides Trap' in international relations is now being played out. This occurs as one superpower (Athens) rises, which creates a fear in the old order (Sparta). The related misunderstandings can lead to war. Thucydides tells us that, in these situations, war is more likely than ever. China, rather than thinking a war vs the US is winnable, is achieving dominance by self-sufficiency, becoming the major nuclear power player, through cyber war and biological warfare. In 2019 the Chinese economy, according to the IMF, was larger than the economies of the three USMCA countries – the US, Mexico, and Canada. China's bypassing of the liberal stage of capitalism, and the jump to authoritarian technocracy, is a huge threat to the rest of the world. The Chinese are asking for a payback from colonialism, and that will entail a military and economic expansion west. Most disturbing is that it is our elites – in executives and legislatures, in our medias and universities – that are the Trojan horse for the Chinese.

China, unlike the Soviet Union, is not attempting to export revolution. China is inculcating the belief that democracy and liberty is for losers and that the brave future of the 'technocrat' millennials is through technology. The Chinese, with their OBOR (One Belt, One Road) initiative is providing the know-how and manpower to reinvent the Silk Road – but this time with all the capital and power flowing one way, across the stans and the citadels, to China. What the US and China share is the way they are prepared to utilise technology to crush dissent. From Cambridge Analytics in the West to Huawei's 'Safe Cities' plan; in Venezuela, Spain, Turkey, Mexico, Serbia, South Africa, Singapore – these nations are utilising Chinese technology to spy and groom their own citizens. What the US is doing *vis a vis* resource-theft in Iraq and Syria, the Chinese are copying the model in the Far East. From Burma to Xinjiang, the Chinese are active in the curtailment of indigenous rights, featuring mass incarceration and re-education camps and population control. However, besides the obvious and belligerent military threat, China is also a health and pollution threat. Covid-19 comes on top of the shocking statistic, post the Paris Agreement, that China is responsible for 48% of continuing emissions. However, vested interests such as Wall Street want to keep China, although Chinese FDI in the US has fallen after its peak in 2016. The new Cold War sees some retrenchment to China in the West, with the likes of the 'Clean Network' initiative of 47 countries to stymie Chinese tech advancement. The technological race will be a lose-lose for the average citizen, who will see freedoms and incomes squeezed on both sides of the new Cold War as military and technological spending eclipses the last vestiges of civil liberties and democracy.

Mao's China started on an industrial revolution and was catching up with Western industrialisation. However, as a power in its region, China has usually been the dominant force. It is through a sustained cultural unity, as well as the obvious economic locomotive, that China is perceived to be such a huge threat. The one thing that China has, which is lacking in the US or the UK, for example, is a homogeneity of culture. This means that China does not sit at the liberal table of multi-culturalism, or dependent upon passages of identity politics. That, in many ways, is its strength. However, a weakness is the lack of pluralism – China has no civil society to offer a buffer to State power. Mandarin as a second language is now displacing English in Asia, and this will be no doubt be accelerated by the rise of the Internet. This is not the global internet, however, as the trend sees various states adopting 'mononet' cultures and restricting access to content. The Chinese homogeneity of culture is seen in the unique public-private nature of the State, which operates in a symbiotic way in the world of business. Unlike in Europe or the US, there is no clear-cut divide. There is not the tension between public and private sector seen in the Occident. The Asian model of democracy proclaims a singular unified state in which human rights take a back seat in the new material-driven version of Confucianism. Unity is a far more important driver of culture than any equivalent in the West; in fact, the Chinese consider their culture a superior one to be extrapolated abroad. The cultural turn which the world must make is the revaluation and integrity of civil society, bereft of petty single-issue divisions, and a return to devolved states, small state, and a spiritual reinvigoration of ethics based on truth. An economic decoupling from China is the long-term goal in the fight against pandemics and barbarism. Whilst the Chinese colossus may seem all-encompassing, there is, like with the Soviet Union, an internal tension. What China lacks, however, is a coherent moral telos. Authoritarian technocracy, Confucianism, and consumerism, are welded together as a whole despite of history, forgetting the purpose of existence, resulting in the alienation of the individual.

Not only is there a contraction of world macro-politics to micro-politics, but there are schisms within the western nation states themselves. In the US, the demarcation is between the urban government workers of the cities, and the knowledge workers – or the 'New Class', as political scientists call them. On the other side of the fence is a Southern Bible Belt grouping of white working-class and middle-class suburb dwellers, who see the rise of the urban caucus as essentially removed from the realities of traditional working communities. It is, therefore, not only a cultural divide but also a geographical one. *The Big Sort: Why the Clustering of Like-Minded America Is Tearing Us Apart,* by Bill Bishop and Robert G. Cushing,[4] illustrates how the US is clustering in same communities as they increasingly feel alienated with the other. This was elevated to extreme partisan aggressivity, as shown in the 2020 US election debacle – a polarisation which feeds into the elites' requirements in a divide-and-rule mindset. These tendencies reflect the priorities of the metropolitan elites, entitled to the benefits of government, public sector money, and ignoring a chunk of the population who exist within real economies. However, the Confederacy, it must be noted, which occupied an area the size of Europe, monopolised the main constituent of trans-Atlantic trade – cotton. Consequently, large swathes of the geographic south are in fact the economic bulwark of the US. They also had the military strength to provoke disunion. Yet the natural state of liberalism is now economic entrepots, and a continuing division of societies on economic, geographic, racial, and identity lines. Community based on shared values, citizenship, and an underlying telos, has been relegated by factionalism promoted by the tech giants and medias. The new technological elites see the vast majority of citizens as mere worker ants, whilst the elites pursue globalised politics and wealth creation. The elites see affinity to a self-styled tech and bureaucratic class which is extra-national; these people often work in governmental organisations, NGOs, World Bank, and EU institutions, which are hugely removed from the practical experiences of ordinary people. A devolution to more localised democratic communities, without deference to urban powers, is more practical. The public-private represents an increasingly empowered and liberal state sector which appears, to ordinary working-class people, as divorced from the realities of economic recession or Covid. These processes will transmute into increasing divisions and tensions based around spiralling national debt. In the US, a process of 'soft disunion' between the metropolitan elites' urban strongholds and HL Mencken's Bible Belt expanse is underway. In the UK, the incompetence of government (due to the inefficacy of centralised authoritarianism) will see the devolution process worked out in a United Ireland and Scottish Independence. The contraction of globalised ideology, if not the sudden contraction of globalised trade, and a devolution of power to the peripheries, means a reversion to a more fundamental sensibility and control over ethical and moral paths.

The Strange Death of Liberalism

When Marc Chagall painted the characters of his metaphysical world in Belarus, his paintings were revolutionary and hard to pigeon-hole. They transcended the now, and faced the stony criticism of conservatives. People and objects are seen upside down, tumbling into space; it represented that iconoclastic time of the Russian Revolution, turning the values of the world on its head. The post-Coronavirus epoch feels like one of those stages of history when iconoclasts can claim new ideas, new directions. However, that turn is the spectre of liberalism writhing in its final death throes; this can be seen in the hotly-contested Biden election 'victory', where the transparency of voting was called into question and the streets swathed in animosity. This can be seen in the collapse of universalism and globalisation; a realisation of the antithesis of liberal philosophies with those of the 'individual'. We have seen how the modern world has displanted the community and family from life. This was achieved through the elevation of the individual as a private atomised actor. Before the Industrial Revolution, life was framed through the intimate family. The family acted as a community; it provided care for the old, a method of informal policing, and also in the economic sphere with perhaps work on the farm or in the municipal guild. The family operated as a *de facto* bank, in the sense that family members would draw on unofficial loans or barter services to extend the mill, the farm, or the blacksmiths. It is worth noting that the institutions to which we give allegiance – the State and Police – are 'imagined communities'; an aggregation of individuals which do not correspond to 'real' communities.

In the liberal era, the market and the State have replaced these traditional bonds of kinship. The individual has tried to find his place in a constructed community. Typically, an actor may work in a large multinational and pay his taxes to an anonymous Inland

Revenue. By contrast, pre-industrial societies probably accounted for monetised payments of approximately 10%; most work and reciprocal barter exchange was done in a tight-knit community with traditional roles and allegiances. The strength of the Chinese Ming dynasty was the 'Baojia' system of 100 families, which were responsible for collecting taxation for the titular state. There was no conception, theoretically or practically, of the notion of the individual. Now the individual has substituted the family and community for the State and market. This is particularly important for liberalism, for, unlike other political philosophies such as fascism and communism, there is no loyalty to a fatherland or a class. Liberalism works by uprooting individuals from family and community for the sake of the market; hence the massive levels of social discord. Likewise, the idea of globalisation works by uprooting the national state into a world economic system, without the shackles of the community and without the shackles of the nation state; globalisation was the ultimate neo-capitalist experiment. However, the failure of the idea has been spectacularly illuminated in the Coronavirus tragedy. Individuals realise that the present nation state is unable to protect them from external global shocks. This is because states are linked to powerful international actors who have no interest in unprofitable activities or funding the intermittent crises. Increasing knowledge, despite the manipulation of medias, has given people the opportunity to see the essence of the virus crisis, and the realisation that the crisis is not a technical one but an ideological one. Pandemics illuminate the normal, dormant problems often hidden in statistics or government debt.

Family and community have been replaced by a technological and bureaucratic liberalism; it is given a veneer of democratic authenticity with representative democracy, but the main requisite is the efficient running of financial markets, banking, and speculative investment. During the Coronavirus contraction of 2020, whilst health workers and key workers struggled to meet the incessant demand of death, speculative hedge fund managers celebrated astonishing betting pay-outs. Ruffer Investment, a

London-based hedge fund, announced in April 2020 a profit of 2.6 billion Dollars over the Coronavirus period so far. 'Universa Investments Fund' in the US made a profit of 3612% during the period up to April 2020. Liberalism becomes an economic philosophy based also on a strong ideological component. For the ideology of neo-liberal markets is based on the need for dysfunctional labour – labour which is deunionised, freelance (gig economy), and in constant tension. Economists use the term 'optimal level of unemployment' for a reason; it is usually around 6-7%, and that contributes to a buoyant, keen, and pliable workforce. Liberalism is an ideological construct because it starts from a premise; a premise of inequality.

Some economists have spoken of ways to reduce child poverty in countries by making large benefits payments to the urban poor, say 75% of the average wage (basic income). This would result in a Keynesian-type stimulation effect as predicted, but also the 'multiplier' economic effect of boosting other industries and, hence, other economies. It would also ensure the lifting from poverty of working-class children born into benefits poverty. The main reluctance to implement such a redistributive scheme is not based on economics (i.e. inflation) but based on ideology. It is the ideology of individualism, of difference, of a market economy of value. Middle England position themselves in relative economic terms to the other. As in Ferdinand Saussure's linguistic definition of the 'sign', words only have meaning in relation to others. A word on its own has no meaning. People in liberalism define themselves as an economic sign, positioned against another. Liberalism submerges the individual in the universalism of the liberal world view, hence the individual struggles for *authentic identity* in the globalist constructs, visible through incessant sex (gender), ethnicity, etc, narratives. End of History narratives, Adam Smith-type market inevitabilities, take over from choice and freedom and empowerment. Political leaders become, within liberalism, careerists rather than philosophes. The modern ideal of the bureaucrat replaces the visionary, in the way rationalism of the Enlightenment replaced the Church. This is coordinated through greater and greater technological decision-making – in all spheres, even war. Technology replaces the real immediate with the atomised virtual world.

We have seen a movement away from reality to one of virtual reality; in most spheres of life, human beings are increasingly divorced from nature, environment. Liberalism promised what Weber described as the 'demystification of the world' – a reaction to the Divine Right of Kings and the monarchical regimes of Europe. Reason replaced God, but has offered up only a technological and rational economic system. In effect, liberalism, despite the promises of Kantian freedom, has placed the majority of world homo sapiens into indentured slavery. The effects of the Coronavirus shock offer a few pathways forward. Most liberal commentators speak of recessions, a breakdown or retrenchment from globalised markets. However, deglobalisation needs to be met with a new philosophy which places people back into community and sanctifies the family. In this way, a new spirituality – divorced from monotheism which corrupted the spirituality of the past – can be an unexpected benefit of a more caring, communal, and spiritual ontology. The modern era has rejected any form of philosophical freedom (spirituality) and has had technology imposed on individuals, regardless of choice. This is illustrated in the bifurcation of man/machine which has taken over the liberal ontology. The modern period has seen the disassembling of man from natural ontology – from being. Heidegger asserted that technology in the modern epoch replaced authentic being, but replaced it with nihilism. This accounts for the profound sadness and isolation one witnesses within modern societies, as we saw with Philip Alston's UN report on the UK. Historians and political theorists maintain that there are three political theories: Fascism, Marxism, and Liberalism. It would be fair to say that all these theories have been hugely discredited for the myriad of reasons we have highlighted in this book. Likewise, their names have become discredited due to the historical associations.

It is difficult to find or use a new term to describe the constitution of what could be called 'Syncretism' to describe the core tenets of the theory. Syncretism represents aspects of a new formulation which incorporates a plethora of themes from tradition and modernity, but the devolution of power, small-scale agriculture, municipal-scaled democracy, and direct participation, degrowth and deglobalisation, environmental safeguards/abolition of certain industries, i.e. chemicals. It would mean the abolition of the World Bank, IMF, the EU, and globalised government. It would mean a move to self-sufficiency in farming, and humane food supplies. It would elevate animals back to an equal footing with homo sapiens; before Kantian rights, theorists consigned them to the horrors of industrialised farming. Syncretism is not left or right; it is important to move away from the language of the elites and to look objectively at issues without the framing effects of medias and the abuse of language.

Liberalism takes a paternalistic view of servitude; the State would guarantee all in exchange for your liberty. This would mean indentured work or benefit payments – the upshot being 'dependency' enforced by the authoritarian aspects of the police state. What the liberal left aspires to achieve is dependency. Dependency is dressed up in the vernacular of benefits, welfare programs, but entails the enlargement of the State and civil servants at the expense of real economies and real freedoms. The working-class dependent on benefits are easy to control. In 1966, two Sociology professors at Columbia, Richard Cloward and Francis Fox Piven, wrote a paper called 'The Weight of the Poor: A Strategy to End Poverty', which involved an attempt to introduce a collectivism in order to paralyse the US Economy in the wake of incessant social anomie. Through the suffocation of the American welfare system by demand, the plan was to bring down the federal structure. The federal government, they thought, would be compelled to introduce a far more centralised system of benefits, and therefore... control. What the new Democrat liberal policy wishes to attain is a new supra-dependency; the majority of working -class people as the worker ants for a nomenklatura of Identity groups devoid of normal work capabilities. The new privileged groups extract money from a benevolent public and corporate sector. Benefit dependency has been shown to create a toxic concentration of power in State operatives, and this was the main hope of the Cloward-Piven Plan, as it was called. John McWhorter, in his book, *Winning the Race: Beyond the Crisis in Black America*, maintained that the welfare strategy has 'created generations of black people for whom working for a living is an abstraction'.[1] What liberals require is the subjugation of working class people -whilst the elites organise, control and spend the surplus. Identity Politics becomes commodified as a vehicle to control adversarial groups.

Dependency has been facilitated by the nature of Federal Reserve spending (printing money) and a spiralling debt problem. However, debt monetisation means that the real purchasing power of the currency fades; since 1972, the dollar has lost 98% of its purchasing power. Meanwhile, dependency on food stamps and benefits has increased from 25 million to 50 million people, all in the space of ten years. In general, the attempt is to generate a 'big state' where the poor and civil servants are invested with stake-holding in the system and the State. It has worked in the UK. A weak and fragile working-class population, dependent on Tony Blair's paternal model of socialism, with a State sector co-opting some of the working-class. Now, in the US, it is an attempt to move the US away from concepts such as freedom and democracy. The Coronavirus shock has catapulted these elements forward, using the Trojan horse of the Democratic Party to gain power. A $2 trillion-dollar bailout, huge increases in welfare recipients, is good ground for the transformation. In a striking dialectic, the Coronavirus is proving to be Lenin's 'Iskra' (spark) for the liberal left.

Whilst the media have been advocating the existence of institutional racism following a series of incidents *vis a vis* Police brutality, there appears to be a myopic ignoring of other issues. The late 90s witnessed a catastrophic attack on the health of white working-class Americans. Nicholas Eberstadt, chair of Political Economy at the American Enterprise Institute, has outlined a massive health crisis amongst America's white working-class. Between 1999 and 2015, there were massive spikes in mortality for the age groups between 25 and 64. Men and women in their fifties saw death rates jumping by 22%. They jumped by 90 per cent for young men in their thirties. Death rates were attributed to 'poisonings' (the euphemism for drug overdoses, mostly opiates), cirrhosis of the liver, and suicide. Excess deaths were in the hundreds of thousands. There were no notices in the media, no features on CNN, and the Clinton, Bush, and Obama administrations said and did... nothing.

During the Cold War, however, US statisticians were quick to notice a similar trend in the Soviet Union. Why the echelons of the US elites failed to mention their own catastrophe indicates the disdain with which these metropolitan apparatchiks hold the white working-class. Social Policy also failed to recognise similar health disasters within the disenfranchised ethnic minorities of US cities. Eberstadt cites a huge lacuna in government information – a complete lack of statistics on health, crime, homelessness, the family. The real net worth of the bottom half of American society was lower before the onset of Covid than when the Berlin Wall collapsed. Employment rates for men in 2019 were worse than the period of the Great Depression. A cursory glance at these statistics would suggest that America's elites, of Trump or Obama, have little interest in a certain section of the population. The essence of liberalism was the removal of attachments of responsibility; at first, this was reflected in a type of liberation ideology, removing oneself from the shackles of the Church, the family, and now the nation state. This was accompanied by a transferral of power to anonymous institutions promising Human Rights and global governance, but at the further erosion of community. As in Marxism, where the individual gives up family/community allegiance to the assurances of a singular class and state, so liberalism promised reciprocity through the benefits of market capitalism. However, as we saw, this form of social contract has reached its zenith with the decline in economic growth and the rise in global inequalities. We were in a period of post-modernism which now has evolved into the 'end of politics'. Liberalism's last stand has morphed into a post-Marxist cultural settlement. This was seen in the philosophies of superstructures which replaced economic determinism; the assumption on the intellectual left that the working-class had somehow lost their way, engulfed in consumerism. It meant the substitution of economics with culture. Gramsci and Marcuse were the harbingers of an elitist model of Marxist thought which attempted to battle with the apparent contradiction that working-class people liked cars, TVs, and could accept a level of oppression from the State. The solution was a top-down approach which advocated the infiltration of the hegemony, into government, State institutions, academia, and the media.

The quintessence of this liberal diaspora is seen in the attraction of these cultural actors to movements such as Black Lives Matter; in essence, the liberal left has abandoned traditional economic concerns for the pyrrhic victories of identity politics. That identity politics is race-based only serves, however, to push native working-class communities towards nation state politics. The culmination of this long march through the institutions is the divisive radical movement of 2020 – a movement born of frustration and agenda-driven modes such as feminism and Black Lives Matter. The essence of this liberal milieu has moved the debate to perceived grievances based on ethnicity and policing, and away from universal themes of inequality. The Democrats in the US and the Labour Party in the UK, however, have failed to note the drift away from identity by other ethnic groups, most notably Asians and Hispanics who, for cultural reasons, do not wish to identify with insubstantial divisive mantras. Therefore, whilst the new radical identity politics which underpins the new liberalism may stem from some fundamental grievances, it has created a radical new schism. The attack on neo-liberalism and globalised markets has ended the traditional belief in 'E pluribus Unum' amongst the liberal left of the sixties, to one of intolerance and an adoption of the UK model of unequivocal multiculturalism. That is, an ideological rejection of civic duty or participation – the philosophy of Martin Luther King – to a conception of unaccountable citizenship. In France the integrationist model of multi-culturalism demands more of its citizens. Hence the move towards race-orientated identity politics which asserts rights above a common-sense citizenship, a feature of nativist working-class communities, will only increase existing divisions within already splintered communities.

There have been essentially three types of revolution. There has been the democratic revolution: the long march of the Magna Carta, Cromwell, the French Revolution, the US constitution, the Suffragettes, to name but a few. This has been an embryonic process, as democratic ideas morph and twist their way to the present continuum. This was accompanied by a second type of revolution – the economic. This was an Industrial Revolution which fundamentally altered homo sapiens' relationship with nature and family and community. This, however, was seen as a movement away from dark, feudal practice. It was an economic revolution, with an attempt to modernise production and farming for the political elites of the merchant classes and the new middle classes of urbanised Europe. The third type are what we call 'cultural revolutions'. History has seen few cultural revolutions. Most revolutions are, in essence, an attempt to usurp power relations *vis a vis* Pareto's idea of the circulation of elites. There are very few grassroots revolutions. The Iranian Revolution was one; Liberation Theology in Latin America, another. They were genuine concerns by working-class actors, merged with a religiosity which questioned the inequality of elite rule. However, the third type of revolution is what has occurred recently. The Black Lives Matter movement can be termed in the third class of revolutions – that of cultural revolution. These revolutions seek a fundamental, rapid shift in the make-up of civil society, and are not merely a recirculation of elites as in political revolutions. They are grand schemes: Mao's cultural revolution; Pol Pot's return to the countryside in Kampuchea. The problem with cultural revolutions, like messianic cults, is that they become obsessive around singular themes. Mao and Pol Pot had a messianic belief in a peasant-based agricultural revolution, a form of agrarian communism. During the Robespierre terror there were executions of priests and a worshipping of reason; Mao's agricultural cultural revolution starved to death up to 50 million people. In Kampuchea, children were brainwashed to report on their parents. These types of revolutions lack a cultural or political nuance – that is the ability to merge the past and present. They are iconoclastic and retributional.

We see the Black Lives Matter social protests toppling statues but lacking a pluralistic supporter base, emphasising a narrow conception of civil society. It is not a political revolution, as it only maintains support of a section of the elite until the elites themselves feel threatened. Cultural revolutions can only be sustained by themselves resorting to a dictatorial or messianic leader, such as Pol Pot or Stalin. Nevertheless, there are some similarities between Mao's revolutionary cadre and the disenfranchised university student body of the BLM movement. The attraction to Mao was their essential naivety and their replacement of expertise with rhetoric. Even revolutions need an articulate and skilled government. The present 'revolution' is essentially cathartic in nature; an attempt to find a sense of moral righteousness from a society which has foregone any moral imperative. Mao's cultural revolution published a list of 400 films for criticism, and there are similarities in the US liberal harassment of teachers, artists, corporate giants, writers, etc, to accommodate their views to the revolution. The 'long march through the institutions' by liberal activists in academia, government, and the media, has given another path, outside of the ballot box, to the attempt at accessing the US nomenklatura. However, cultural revolutions are different to political or working-class revolutions. Mao's cultural revolution in China is misleading, as it was, in essence, a top-down orchestrated attempt to solidify power. In fact, many of the key players who travelled to rural China came back with sanguine ideas about Mao's agricultural utopia.

However, in opposition to cultural revolutions of the liberal sort, we have now what are called the rise of 'Civilisational States'. Up until now, we have had what the Germans call *Machtstaat* (the mighty power state) in the guise of the US, Soviet Union, and China. They saw themselves as a guiding light for world affairs. Other peripheral states, such as the UK, France, etc, believe they are in the mould of the old liberal tradition of *Rechsstaat* (a rule of law state). These states enshrine, or believe they do, the notions of human rights and liberty. The civilisational states, which can be seen in Russia, Iran and also India, Pakistan are, in essence, guardians of tradition and conservative. They tend to emphasise a particular tradition (i.e. orthodox Christianity, Hindu India). Hence, we have, in the new era, a parallel process; the retreat to nation states in the guise of a reconstituted Westphalian order and the demise of globalisation. But at the same time, we have new actors on the civilisational stage, with huge public support. The civilisational states are the antithesis to liberal democracies. They, rightly or wrongly, see the values of the liberal world as corrupting. The mistake of the liberal left is to dismiss these actors as 'backward' and judge them through their own *kulturbrille*. Civilisational states embody more of the values of tradition and a spiritual ontology. By their very nature they are suspicious of globalised or ahistorical narratives. In contrast to the Occidental view of life, the civilisational states place heroism and spirit in front of the market and the individual. By contrast, the 'Technological Age' of globalisation sees its 'progress' as the continuing obliteration of the individual into technological forms.

Syncretism: Community and Spirit

Modernism has compartmentalised belief through the internet – a new 'pick and mix' religiosity which has been transformed, mostly, into social justice memes and products. The new beliefs spring up from what Durkheim recognised in religions as a set of beliefs and practices which give the individual a sense of community. That, of course, would be a sociologist's view, but it has merit. The atomisation of the individual has led to a similar seeking for identity. The internet has allowed the individual to custom build his/her portfolio of beliefs. Here, religiosity has been transferred into a consumerist virtual world of affiliation in which commitment and experience can be downloaded in an instant. However, the atomised millennial is not really 'choosing' their religion. With the efficiency of algorithms, Google, and Cambridge Analytics, religiosity and community are now engineered and sold. What appears as choice is the signification of what the elites have programmed for the new millennials. What is missing is what Peter Berger called the 'sacred cosmos' – religion as a philosophical experience, a *bildungsroman* of life, from the curtains raised to the denouement, full of epiphanies and horrors.

The most virulent form of the new progressivism, and which gives the appearance of a type of transcendence, is the social justice/anti-racism movements. The salvation goal becomes the eradication of police brutality/institutional racism, etc. However, redemption never seems to satisfy, and social justice leaps from one movement to the next in the endless quest for that lost identity. The virtue world becomes quickly commodified: BLM t-shirts, LGBTQ pop cans. There is a symbiotic commercialism as corporate brands monetise social justice and then are themselves obliged to fund, promote, and adapt in a virtual cohabitation.

The end game of globalisation, of the technological society, is the atomisation of the individual within a functioning Weberian bureaucratic and economic system. For that reason, the demonisation of religions, the curtailment of 'free thinkers', the persecution of off-grid and libertarian communities, is evidence for the increasing domination of the 'supra-state'. These 'others' are demonised, as mentioned earlier, by the media and the establishment's monopoly on language. They are 'terrorists', 'communists', 'cults', 'anarchists'. The Suffragettes were accused of being anarchists, unfeminine, etc; any group which upsets the establishment, which disputes the discourse of the metropolitan elites, is described in such terms. The 'individual' is a much-confused term. We tend to think of individualism as a positive thing, and it is – but not in the modern epoch where there are no individuals, only what the German language calls *gesellschaften*, which are societies, an aggregation of individuals. What modern society has lost is what Heidegger calls *gemeinschaft* – a complete feeling of community. The effects of this can be seen in the texture and dysfunctional nature of British and US society. We are thrown into an existential world of conflict and alienation, since the present organisation of economic and cultural norms do not correspond to the historical nature of homo sapiens.

Ideas of community, or a good community, presuppose however, a type of ethical view, a set of moral virtues which are set from innate forms or laws. In *After Virtue*,[1] Alisdair MacIntyre argues that ordinary social 'practices' and 'goods internal to practices' need to be protected against their corruption from 'institutions', which seek the 'external goods' of power, money, etc. Virtue comes from the teleology of a culture, not – as in Enlightenment thinking, – from the subjective individual. Man cannot escape the past, for it defines him. Rather than the atomised individual of the Enlightenment, humans are part of a shared tradition. Despite this, modern liberalism expects man to exist as a collection of strangers, with the individual creating a lone path but with the caveat of working for a rationalised economic system. The two ideas cause the tension of precarity and isolation we witness in liberal societies. Consequently, notions of justice or virtue float in a vacuum, as they must be anchored in a coherent goal-oriented community system. The discussions of justice, therefore, are moored in reason; however, using scientific principles to address moral discussions is meaningless. Certainly, reason came out of tradition, but is not the sole criteria for forming societal relations, legal systems, or economic theories. However, the Enlightenment belief in reason was then rejected by Nietzsche as relativistic morality, and this set the tone for the nihilistic philosophies of Sartre, etc, in the twentieth century. The task, as I see it, is to rebuild some kind of moral framework, not necessarily 'religious' *per se* but based on community and spirituality. Although Nietzsche was right to expose the hypocrisy of religious fundamentalism and the herd mentality of mass society, he did not offer up a virtuous analysis of how to act. Frazer, in his *The Golden Bough*, showed how magic morphed into spirituality and into organised religion, that religion is a harking back to an 'Eden', an eternal return to conceptions of a paradisiacal garden, as in Islamic thought. The Western occidental tradition stems from a deep-rooted history of Greek, Roman, and Christian thought. A more useful approach is a synthesis of ideas, a meeting on the Silk Road, a sifting of ideas into a useful hybrid, devoid of the falsification of language.

Therefore, it is a search for a form of ethics for the modern world. The search for meaning can be seen in Christianity, Judaism and Islamic approaches worldwide, although they suffer from the same uniform thinking mentioned previously, lacking synthesis with other ideas, the quagmire of faith. Whilst there are no true scientific constants, there are paths of virtue, ethics, and goodness, passed down from archaic and indigenous communities. The problem since the Enlightenment has been the dismantling of the notions of ethics, which have reached their pinnacle in modern liberal democratic capitalism. The Enlightenment based its reason on the subjective principles and the individual, whilst the Aristotelian idea of the telos actuated a state that humans should aspire to. An example we could give is that of the Easter Islanders. For some religious reason, they started upon a series of statue building which eventually led to the catastrophic destruction of their environment. What they had done was to abandon the moral teleology which had underpinned previous generations of thought.

It is a common occurrence in the destruction of societies. But it was not merely an ecological problem. The existing metalanguage was abandoned for the new way of living, based on the worship of statues. The incoherent nature of the switch condemned them to disaster. As Kahneman notes, we tend to be experts at describing the logical series of events of the past; with hindsight, we apply a naive reasoning to epic events and look for these patterns in the future. For example, the Enlightenment was the destruction of superstition and the 'dark ages'. Of course, reality is more nuanced, more cryptic. The switch to Enlightenment thinking was thus based on similar incoherent principles, and removed the conception of 'good' to the realm of the individual and replaced it with scientific reason, irrespective of the traditions of archaic and community traditions. Likewise, the advent of industrialisation was based on an incoherent departure from a tradition or community. Again, the advent of modern technological society has witnessed the separation of the individual from notions of community, and enmeshed them into the singularity of technological faith. The community provides the only necessary social system for meeting humans weaknesses and frailties. The destiny of the human is not Nietzsche's *Ubermensch* but a community of values based on the idea of 'renaissance man' rather than post-Enlightenment industrialised man.

The Eclipse of the Enlightenment

Certain epochs require scapegoats to define the legitimacy of political (and military) action, to define public policy. In Tsarist Russia, the regularity of anti-Jewish pogroms coincided with times of famine, political upheaval, and crisis – a diversionary tactic to blame the other. In the post-World War 2 arena, Communism and the Soviet Union were the pariah default scapegoats. The logic was simple: a philosophy which limited the spread of free enterprise, and therefore limited the markets available for the pursuance of mass consumerism and the neo-liberal agenda. States which disrupted the flow of capital were demonised – Vietnam, Nicaragua, Cuba.

The new pariahs are Islam and Christianity because, essentially, they represent some of the core values which are the antithesis of global consumerism: equality, family, community, and freedom within civil society. Of course, the constant mantra of the West is to demonise Islam as 'fanatical' and 'intolerant'; it rewards elites in Islamic countries which play the game – Saudi Arabia, UAE, etc. However, these states are as far away from the core beliefs of Islam as is the present US government, in comparison with the founding fathers of the US Constitution. The rise in the popularity of Islam is a direct corollary of the impact of materialism on these countries; the rise in fundamentalist Islam is a result of encroachment of materialism on the core tenets of belief – family and community. Therefore, the vociferous motifs of post-Enlightenment civil society in the West – individualism and representative democracy – do not fit easily into Islamic society. Religion in Islamic society provides the political philosophy of the State; therefore, a state which includes an element of spirituality in its public policy will have other issues at the heart of its *raison d'etre*. The concomitant rise in the idea of the 'Nation State' in Europe, from the nineteenth century onwards, was a necessary precursor to the marginalisation of community and religion. The nation state was a useful structure to administrate capital, to evoke a new feeling of 'pseudo-community' at the expense of real communities at a local level. What we need is the devolution to smaller entities, based on Westphalian principalities. It is important to reiterate the point of 'imagined communities', because it is especially central to modern capital. Loyalty comes from bonds based on archaic principles of love, community, cooperation, and spirituality. The modern state has replaced this with the Weberian bureaucratic state. Globalisation requires the eradication of community, of familial bonds. Therefore, the post-Enlightenment ideas of Adam Smith, Locke, and Hegel are couched in 'institutionalised' community and individual freedoms. So, freedom is seen through the lens of the legal apparatus.

However, social justice was the emblem of traditional Islam, but social justice under the aegis of the just ruler. But human agency, the march of the individual, were seen to be absent in an old-fashioned Islam. So Western critics and philosophers see civil society as largely a European development; a lack of pluralism in Islam, a weakness. However, this overeggs the way Islam is seen through an 'Orientalist' lens, and ignorant of grass roots movements. But mostly it sees civil society through the viewpoint of Western ideas of freedom and democracy. Together with this is the paucity of inflicting Western economic and political institutions on the Islamic world; it is on a different metaphysic. However, the thinking covers development and the paternalistic governance of institutions involved in spreading the 'good word'. The Western civil society paradigm was likewise hoisted upon post-Soviet CEE states, and also South American countries such as Brazil, Argentina, and Chile. Surely these communities would want a different civil society with the influence of Buddhist, Orthodox, Catholic clusters? This endemic disease in thinking is common in the European Commission, the World Bank, and the development organisations. Western civil society has a multiplicity of problems; they are illustrated in the current contradictions in civil society in the West, where groups compete for resources and space with zero cooperation. The French and UK multi-cultural failure is based on the idea that various ethnic groups can participate side by side only in economic relations. The experience of Pakistanis in the UK, Moroccans in France, Turks in Germany, is evidence for tensions related to this. This is not to say that peoples cannot share the same space. They do, and they can – but not when the only common denominator is for them to provide the workforce for neo-liberal capitalism.

Samuel Huntington called the confrontation of liberal democracy and the 'developing' world of Islam as a 'clash of civilisations'. It is also the myopic thinking of populist nationalist leaders in the West who denigrate Islam. This does not stand up to any warranted historical explanation. When the Silk Road meandered through ancient civilisations, through the minarets of Samarkand, through the endless sands of the Dasht e Kavir desert in Persia and onto the caravanserais of Tabriz, there was no clash, but an attempt at a synthesis of ideas, from the Buddhist Chinaman to the Islam of Central Asia. The motif of the caravanserai, the hospitable inn with its paradisiacal fountain, stretched brightly across the way, and Christian, Platonic ideas flowed one way and Buddhism and Islam the other. The caravanserais were ostensibly a trade route, but people exchanged ideas, philosophies, and faiths. Now the Silk Road is awash with borders, bombs, and US military bases. Ignorance is almost a byword for the media view of Islam. The heartland of Islam is conceived as the Middle East, but the majority of Muslims live in India, Pakistan, and Indonesia. Islamic countries are mostly termed in a Western paradigm – 'developing nations'. Developing to what? The real answer is developing according to the standard US and European model – the market economy. A common reference point for judging the performance of state and civil society are the indicators given by the Human Development Index (HDI), which measures quantitative data rather than qualitative. Norway regularly tops the list. The UK falls way behind a plethora of nations such as Switzerland, Ireland, Germany, Hong Kong, Iceland, etc. Of course, the main indicators are income per capita, life expectancy, and education. These are not qualitative factors which most ordinary people can gauge, i.e. what is a country 'like'? What do its citizens consider good or bad, etc? Therefore, the HDI only represents the Western paradigm of thinking: GDP, growth, per capita income. For example, it does not reflect non-State-controlled factors, i.e. community health and education, grassroots democratic movements, communal life, independent media, sports participation, cultural groups (dance, poetry, music, etc). Again, the definition of political life is defined by the HDI as 'electoral'. It ignores rural communities where informal neighbourhood networks exist. For example, in Nepal, the Magyar people do not have (do not need) the concept of a 'police' force, as disagreements are dealt with through peer pressure and discussion. There is no formal healthcare system, but the Shaman of a village knows an extensive cornucopia of medicinal plants located in the environment.

The Iranian revolution was an egalitarian grass roots movement combined with Islamic traditions, not a *coup d'état* by a few mad mullahs. It was precisely the ideas of religious philosophy within the Quran which enabled the Shah to be overthrown. In fact, the petrochemical incursions into these countries led to increased levels of inequality there. The Arabic and Persian language for civic organisations long pre-dates the recent Western notions of civil society: for example, *'mujtama al-madani'*, *'jame'eh madani'*. The premise that 'individualism', the obsession with elections, the levels of social dysfunctionality of the West, are a reflection of a high level of civil society, is merely the twisted view from the Occident. There is a much deeper sense of civil society in so-called developing nations. There is a community-informed element of the teleology of purpose, and that is why Aristotelianism was taken up by the Islamic philosophers of the Medieval period. When Islam sprang from the Arab heartland of Mohammed, it had inherited the tribal traditions of the Arabs; it was an egalitarian creed. When Muslims prostrated themselves on the floor in prayer, it was a symbol of their nothingness when compared to God. It was necessary to disavow ideas of monarchy, to give 'zakat' to the poor (alms) and to fast at Ramadan in order to feel the suffering of the poor – hence the idea of social justice was an early embodiment of Islam. The idea of the 'ummah' (community) was central to the idea of Islam and more important than 'zannah' – esoteric discussions of faith. Islam was, and is, particularly tolerant of other belief systems, and whilst the spring of Islamic faith rose from Mecca, it was enveloped in a poor and limited agriculture.

During the Axial period of the formation of the world religions (approximately from 700BC to 250BC), the religions of affluent areas – for example, ancient Persia, Confucian China, or Byzantium – enjoyed, by contrast, plentiful harvests which nourished the discipline of compassion for the poor. However, this aspect was natural to the Arab, based on tribal virtues, the kind of virtues Lawrence of Arabia admired. So, for Islam, it is impossible to speak of the separation of material life and religion; they are the one and same. The Quran stressed that 'there shall be no coercion in matters of faith' and recognised the same status to the Prophet Jesus, or the Buddha. Hence, if you visit Iran, you see pictures of the Prophet Jesus in hotels and shops. It was Abu Nasr Al-Farabi who died in 950 AD who united Platonic rationalism with Islam. He believed that a Platonic society, with the Imam as 'Philosopher King' could be a focal point for the development of Islam. Al Farabi was a Sufi – an esoteric and spiritual group within Islam – which sought the divine within the individual. This itself was an aesthetic reaction to the development of a legalistic Islam after Mohammed. God could be found in philosophy or within other religious traditions. The import of the pluralism embedded within Islam is important, for it seems to suggest a dichotomy with the West's Occidental view of the religion; it means a re-evaluation of Islamic philosophy and an acknowledgement of the usefulness and synthesis of these ideas. However, whilst the dominant hierarchy of ideas is capitalist and globalised, this dominant discourse needs to demonise core Islamic values which are incompatible with the neo-liberal mantra.

The analogy of the synthetic thinking on the Silk Road illustrates the dynamic way in which religion has in fact been the source of a unification of humankind. Most conventional theories of religion suppose that they are proselytizing and missionary. When people speak of religion, they tend to be talking about organised religion – the cherubs of the Roman Catholic Church, the Church of England. However, before that, religions – from animist beliefs to Shamanic rituals – were localised and had no interest in a mission. In fact, religion for millennia was merely a quest to understand what as human beings we are doing here and why. The agricultural revolution was a disaster for two reasons. Firstly, it relegated animals to second-class status, and started the long horrific march of the animal kingdom at the hands of homo sapiens – a road which will only finish in the extinction of yet another million species of fauna. Secondly, religion was used as a means of fecundity; to ask the gods for help in raising crops. This, as Frazer noted in *The Golden Bough*, moved the spirit from magic to religion and, as the industrial revolution took hold, polytheism moved to monotheism. Polytheism was the belief system which recognised a plethora of gods – for example, the deities of Hinduism: Ganesh, Saraswati. Polytheistic religions were, in general, not missionary or intolerant; the great Polytheistic religions usually incorporated new gods into their nomenklatura. However, it was the advent of Monotheism, the one-God ruler, which signalled the demise of spirituality and tolerance. The infamous religious wars between Catholics and Protestants during the sixteenth and seventeenth centuries killed thousands and thousands of people. However, if you asked Catholic and Protestant communities in Northern Ireland about the theological intricacies of their respective faiths, the majority would be unable to explain the differences. The Catholic emphasis on achieving grace by good deeds seems to have lost its place amongst the golden chalices and incense of Rome. The Protestant Church of England has 'evolved' so much that it seems little different to the views expressed in the *Guardian* newspaper, that repository for everything liberal and atheist.

It was Mircea Eliades who described the division of life into the 'sacred' and the 'profane', so that the ordinary profane world is only real if it reflects the sacred. So, it is similarly akin to searching for the Nietzschean superman in life; therefore Nietzsche, whilst questioning the weak morality of traditional

Christianity, recognised the role of the 'sacred'. Archaic civilisations and the sacred set out the mythic values, and only a harking back to them offers modern man redemption. Modern man has had the umbilical cord with the sacred cut, whilst archaic man uses myths and rituals to return to a mythical age. Therefore, archaic societies view time as cyclical rather than the historicist end of history – that straight arrow of time which materialists are following. Archaic man therefore re-enacts myths, returning to the primordial origins. Consequently, modern man needs to escape the shackles of historical time and this transcendence cannot be done through liberal materialism, as it offers only the profane. Every year, a festival or myth begins again the cycle *ab initio*. Eliades speaks of the 'terror of history', whereby traditional man is seeking to depart from linear historical time by embracing the sacred:

'when historical pressure no longer allows any escape, how can man tolerate the catastrophes and horrors of history—from collective deportations and massacres to atomic bombings—if beyond them he can glimpse no sign, no transhistorical meaning; if they are only the blind play of economic, social, or political forces, or, even worse, only the result of the 'liberties' that a minority takes and exercises directly on the stage of universal history?'[1]

The liberties of the minority here are the liberal democratic elites; it is a pessimistic, nihilist vision, and the only redemption here is to step outside of the trap of history. However, this does not mean necessarily organised religion, but can mean any 'dis-coupling' from modernity. This yearning for the archaic is not an abstract theory for contemporary man. In fact, the longing for spiritual culture can be seen in the culture of the modern world, although it tends to be underground and non-mainstream, in that it is not 'produced' culture but arises from a growing section of society who regard the present paradigm as unsustainable and alien to the platonic rationalism of forms. It is seen in outbursts of archaic patterns; the counter-culture of the 1960s, the New Age offshoots and philosophies, streams of off-grid music and art.

It is also not a utopian wish to return mankind to a perfected Rousseau idea of a state of nature. However, there is an underlying feeling that homo sapiens are divorced from almost every realm of life: production, food, agriculture – all have become a mere extension of technology, with the internet facilitating the political imprisonment of homo sapiens to a technological jailer. Religion as a private field of existence has been replaced by a non-religious and secular credo; this has been disseminated by the liberal corruption of academia, education, and the media. A return to a form of integralism, and a moral, ethics-based limited government, reflecting the values of a transcendent telos, needs to replace empty materialism.

We have seen how societies which depart from their underlying telos or purpose, open themselves to physical and moral decay, and ultimately collapse. Collapse begins from an ideological turn, not a physical one. Government needs to be based on virtues and can take the form of spiritual government, as we have seen within Islam or Catholic integralism. The Enlightenment tragedy was the usurpation of the underlying telos of the worldview by replacing it with rationalism and the autonomy of the individual.

The Owl of Minerva Takes Off

Individuals, and also peripheral societies within globalisation, have lost control over destiny. However, the indicators, accelerated by the Coronavirus shock, have shown that growth has effectively stopped and the rise of income inherent in growth flowed to the top of the tree. For those at the bottom – the majority – income has fallen. Macroeconomic models based on public debt expansion, commodified money, and vacant consumerism, have failed. They failed to predict the GFC of 2008 and have no answers for the Coronavirus impact. Despite their increasing redundancy, these economic paradigms still linger; it is a bit like sitting in the Wuhan market having a bowl of bat soup for the symptoms of Covid-19.

Freakonomics was based on the irrational mythic world of free markets. The reformists – the liberal left leftovers from the Blair/Clinton axis – still talk about reforming capital. They would reform the market with regulation; the mixed economy. Government policy should regulate rent-seeking as a means to wealth. It should promote genuine entrepreneurial wealth. However, it is like constantly fixing that old broken Ford: one minute it's the clutch, then the gearbox, then the engine blows up on Route 66. The neo-liberal method has seen a concentration of firms buying competitors and fixing barriers to entry. Developed liberal democracy means the concentration of power in wealthy corporations and individuals who bankroll elections. It is the apogee of the closing of the political and economic world. These are structural issues so large that painting the old Ford with a pink colour will not suffice. The bird has flown.

The market did not sort everything out. There was no carefully considered scientific, planned response to Coronavirus. The reality was nurses wearing bin bags. We need a replacement of economic indicators with social indicators; GDP does not forecast wealth

171

inequality or corrupted rent-seeking markets. We need the supplanting of GDP with GSP (Gross Social Product). Gross Social Product would see unemployed individuals given useful, interesting social functions within a basic income scenario. Gross Social Product would see local currencies gradually replacing global ones – a move to glocalised markets. Community organisations and clubs would be triumphed. Economic indicators need to account for the depletion of resources and environmental destruction. The tragedy of history is that the 'Owl of Minerva' only takes flight in the dusk. Yet, we have a great opportunity, post-Coronavirus, to reshape the world, equipped with the owls of wisdom. Those owls are not macroeconomic models, but an ideological choice about the type of society which we want. It is one of those seminal moments in history, a pure chance for humanity. Or we can carry on with a Ptolemaic belief in the wisdom of markets. The liberal metropolitan elites need to be removed from constructing oligarchic institutions and 'feminising' weak societies.

There are essentially three paths forward after the Coronavirus impact on the economy and social structures of the world. The first road is the neo-liberal, monetarist (libertarian) philosophy which has caused gross inequalities, political upheavals, and incessant wars. However, even on the American right there is an intellectual move away from this fundamentalist approach. The second path encompasses a wide spectrum from the traditional right. From Catholic professors to company directors; it is a broad church. They embody various nomenklatures such as post-liberal, integralist, traditionalist or conservative. What was framed and sold to the public as the 'new right' – the ideas of Ayn Rand, Adam Smith, Hayek – are now in abeyance. The apogee of conservative monetarism realised that it lacked a fundamental quality or a teleology. That is, there was no moral purpose to the new right beside a confused worship of free markets. In fact, the very labels of left and right are meaningless in the new moral necessities; they exist on a different plane than procedural politics or representative models. Liberalism was essentially an ideological choice to justify inequalities and globalisation. In essence, some of the propositions of conservatism and libertarian markets are incompatible with conservative moral philosophy; for example, issues such as healthcare, Equality Acts, and freedom of speech, etc. The second way is a mix of Social Conservatism. The new philosophies attack the premises of the Enlightenment and liberalism. What has been seen is that the liberalism of the nineteenth century was used as a vehicle to protect the individual, but was really a vehicle to pursue liberal capitalism. The new right had abandoned any moral precepts with liberal views on family, abortion, etc. So, the proponents of integralism bring back the Church into the civic politic; it is the conception, akin to Napoleon's idea of a civic religion; the embedding of catholic ideas in the State (rather than the superiority of the secular state). Therefore *'summum bonum'* replaces the anarchy of the market. Therefore, it is, besides the imposition of a moral theology, at essence the same system of economic and social relations; that is, it still works within the existing paradigm. On the global stage, the new schema would advocate small state nationalism (principalities) rather than imperialism, a retreat for US foreign policy. Speculative capitalism in the US has deepened inequalities. However, it is not only a battle between worker and elites; the new battleground is also between a small group of super-rich (0.1%) and the traditional realms of America's top 10%. What has occurred, through a mix of automisation and 'elite overproduction', has been an unemployment debacle for America's middle classes, especially graduates. This social disaffection is seen in the 2020 rioting and violence aimed at predominantly Democratic jurisdictions in the US. These new graduates, often in liberal disciplines, find themselves unwanted and unqualified.

Eeconomic policy favours a new 'Industrial Policy', as in Germany or Japan, to boost the economy. This second coming of 'Conservative Capitalism', infused with catholic sensibilities, has gathered pace amidst the Coronavirus maelstrom. The need for a rational, organised state seems necessary in times of woe, and it is abundantly clear that present structures of globalised government cannot react or plan efficiently. However, as we have seen, neither can national governments. It could be argued that private-public initiatives, such as the Bill Gates one, may be the way forward – which would indicate more of a libertarian view of the State. Whatever the view, bureaucratic structures and their inefficiency have been the hallmark of many countries during the Coronavirus pandemic. All approaches, whether from Milton Friedman's 'Helicopter Money' to George Soros's proposal for perpetual bonds for distressed countries, all point to the same schema – Keynesian inflations. It proves that the monetarism of Milton Friedman was wrong in an economic way, even above and below its clear social disaffection. However, 'Industrial Policy' stimulus must be productive- geared towards small industries and entrepreneurs in real commodities; rather than pumping money into the civil service. What we are seeing is the collapse of the notion of the neo-liberal state, of the individual atomised liberal agent, of globalised markets. Nevertheless, both paths of development – the Monetarist and the new Social Conservatism — work in the realms of the same paradigm. They do not approach the issues which are essential for reform. That is: small state devolution to the peripheries; an elevation of family and community; the replacement of fiat currencies with localised currencies to encourage local production; and a system of direct participatory democracy which does not mean the ballot box. Technology and the internet, redirected for socially benevolent means, could quite easily construct a real democratic participatory system. Power is devolved to local groups skilled in particular areas: agriculture, industry, governments of 'Philosopher Kings'. This necessity reflects the history of responses to epidemics like the Coronavirus.

The third possibility here starts from an ideological framework, and that means an assault on the vestiges of inequality. One of the fundamental premises of a new economy is the antithesis of current perceptions of economic growth and GDP. Economic growth is unsustainable. The Industrial Revolution unfortunately started a premise that continued advances in technology and economic growth were the norm. Rather than economic growth being the future, it needs to be realigned to a simple continuum – that of happiness. The way forward is a movement back to community and away from industrialised farming. Industrialised agriculture has destroyed local farming communities; this is also a problem of the concentration of land ownership in the hands of a few. Modern agriculture depends upon extensive use of chemical fertilisers and negates supplies of water and oil. Therefore, the solution is a move to localised small farming, based on a community involving local produced goods and services. Local currencies can be used as a medium of exchange. For example, the scheme in Massachusetts called 'Berkshares' uses a local currency developed by the Schumacher Center for a New Economics. These shares can be traded for local goods and services. The *raison d'etre* behind this is that the currency is shielded against the fortunes of the dollar and macro-economic problems. It means that local communities are not dependent upon the whims of global currency trading and commodity markets; they may be able to suffer external economic shocks such as OPEC oil price hikes and the impact of viruses like the Coronavirus. This results in a multiplier effect in the local economy. Some 400 local businesses participate in the scheme at the moment. The long-term goal is to foster local economic self-sufficiency. It means that local goods will be used instead of imported goods, which are ecologically unsustainable. Imported goods use up fossil fuels and impact the environment. Although the Berkshares are taxed by federal government, it would be an ideal development for them to decouple from national government in this sense. One of the inherent problems is that national governments will be reluctant to give up tax-raising control. The project has been replicated in several other areas and received praise from the likes of *The Economist*. *The Economist* Liveability magazine concurred that, whilst the US has higher disposable income than other countries, it does not translate to happiness. In fact, each generation of Americans is becoming less well off as the real gains are captured by a wealthy few. In a localised system, people will get accustomed to less economic growth; they will trade quantity for quality, and recapture the essence of communities and cooperation. Jobs will become more meaningful as people find solace in help and cooperation, rather than capital accumulation. However, notions such as this need to be replicated on a global continuum – the biggest obstacle being China. The Chinese economic locomotive is a threat to the health and democracy of world nations; a retrenchment from Chinese exports would strangle their economy and the onerous influence it exerts on its neighbours. In fact, the Chinese model is unsustainable *per se*. For example, if the Chinese were to copy American models of car ownership, then there would be an extra one billion cars on the planet. By any reckoning, that is environmentally suicidal. However, the premise here is not that there is a choice between a new paradigm and the traditional growth centred one. It is imperative for economic and equitable reasons that we switch to a sustainable model.

Cuba is an unlikely candidate for a model of agricultural sustainability, but the country which is a byword for the antithesis of neo-liberal economy is now at the forefront of an agricultural revolution. The Cuban revolution under Castro had promised to give the land back to the peasants. The problem was that the market for crops (predominantly sugar cane) was switched off by the US. Unfortunately, Cuba adopted the Soviet approach to agricultural development – heavy mechanised industrial production with chemical fertilisers and pesticides, and the utilisation of machine-centred production rather than people. The State decided on production quotas and a centralised system of control. Despite the negative effects on small-scale farmers, all indicators of education, health, and well-being placed Cuba near the top of lists of comparative success. For example, the WHO Quality of Life Index 1989 had Cuba in eleventh position, whilst the US was fifteenth. However, the demise of Soviet support meant that Cuba lost 50% of food imports. A necessary reconsideration of agricultural policy was on the cards. Therefore, there was a switch to what was called 'Low Input Sustainable Agriculture' (USDA 1980). It was a pragmatic but also a philosophical choice; the reduction in the supply of pesticides forced their hand, but also there was a realisation that traditional agricultural paradigms were destroying the land. The classical model meant 'interdependence', monoculture, and a reliance on heavy machinery and transportation for export. Pesticides and monoculture were exacting a heavy health toll on Cuban people. The key indicators of economies of scale, which had worked under Soviet influence, had become redundant. However, what is seismic about the new Cuban model of bottom-up agriculture is that it restructured not only agriculture, but also the social and economic system. There is an emphasis on research for ecological modes of production and biological pesticides, and the unit of production is brought back to the small-scale freeholder. Scientists use the knowledge of localised farming to research insect management and soil quality. For example, traditional local methods for controlling sweet potato and banana crops using a type of ant has produced a 99% success rate against weevils. Research into plant disease has found that microbial antagonists are highly effective against root diseases on tobacco plants, for example. Crop rotation is used to combat against weed problems; for example, corn can cover and shade low-height weeds, and therefore, beans can be planted the following year. Biological compost is used as an alternative to fertilisers in order to increase soil efficiency. Reforestation and the return of labour to villages and agriculture has been another indicator of the success of Cuba's agricultural revolution. Sara Oppenheim in 'Alternative agriculture in Cuba' writes that:

'By making agriculture essentially a small-scale endeavour on a national level, Cuba has drawn upon local and individual knowledge in designing solutions to problems such as soil fertility and insect management. Revolutionary to their core, Cubans have adopted alternative agriculture as swiftly and passionately as they did the Revolution of 1959. Rather than excluding the populace, the new model in Cuba integrates all areas of society in a common struggle for food self-sufficiency. By asking not if sustainable agriculture is possible, but rather how it can best be carried out, Cuba has paved the way to a more rational form of food production.'[1]

Happy Trails

We saw in an earlier chapter how happiness in the modern world has been manufactured to coincide with material and consumer culture. We are told by the media it takes an average salary of 70,000USD to make one really happy. What then are the real sources of happiness? Martin Seligman in *Authentic Happiness*[1] states that perhaps 50% of happiness has its roots in genetic predilection. Although it is hard to quantify freedom, research has shown a correlation between political freedoms, economic freedoms (what Marx termed 'positive freedom'), and freedom to pursue religious or spiritual goals, lead to increased levels of happiness. Modern Britain has placed a fence around freedoms which have been fought for over centuries. The Race and Religious Hatred Act 2006 and the Equality Act 2010 in the UK have circumscribed speech to the extent that what the Ancient Greeks termed 'parrhesia' (fearless speech) has been outlawed. With technological encroachments in every aspect of life, core freedoms are in retreat. We have also shown that 'representative democracy' is not an indicator of happiness, as the issues highlighted in dysfunctional societies shows. By contrast, research has shown that direct democracy, i.e. in Switzerland (particularly participation in local decision-making), is a more important contributor to happiness than material wealth. In Britain, the centralisation of decision-making and the total absence of citizen empowerment is the direct opposite of libertarian or real democratic societies. Research has also shown the positive effect of personal relationships in forming happiness, especially happy marriages. However, the media bombards young people with rhetoric which demeans the family, marriage, and heterosexual relationships, as if they were 'out of fashion'. Social friendships, societies, and clubs are also a strong source of positive happiness; a fact which has been documented in the US and Britain.

The decline in civic participation in clubs and societies has been well documented, and this trend has had negative consequences for happiness. Robert Putnam's *Bowling Alone* illustrated the general decline in civic community in the US.[2] The individual, like representative democracy, has been atomised, and participatory roles removed. It is reflected in what we saw earlier: decreased voter engagement, public meetings, religious participation, trade unions (labour unions), Scouts, and a wide range of fraternal organisations. The main reason for this is the atomisation of individuals into technological entertainment – computer games, TV, and internet – as they move people away from participatory community. Whilst the State has grown its tentacles into every facet of individual experience, the corollary is diminishing returns from civil society and a break-up of the pluralist models of society which had gained credence in the 60s and 70s. However, we must be careful to stress that this is not the happiness of utility or the CBT (Cognitive Behavioural Therapy) advice advocated by Richard Layard, the 'happiness tsar' of New Labour. Layard in *Can We Be Happier?*[3] correlates data on world happiness studies, and attempts to solve the 'symptoms' of unhappiness – i.e. depression, childhood unhappiness, etc – by advocating policy which attacks these symptoms. For example, he says that a child's happiness is linked to the school he/she attends. This approach fails to look at underlying causes, or the wider picture of societal relations, or the question of 'authenticity', freedom of speech, for example. Layard claims that the problem of unhappiness at work is due to bad bosses. Well, there must be millions of bad bosses then. It has nothing to do with the frosty relationship between labour and capital, or the spiralling alienation we have outlined so far in the neo-liberal world. Layard also claims that marital problems can be solved by CBT provided freely by the State. However, these utilitarian treatments do not go to the core of dislocation politics that the globalised world suffers. China may have brought millions of urban dwellers out of poverty, but that does not make them happy or happier, for it fails to see that it is inequality and culture which are core contributors to unhappiness.

Religion is another great source of happiness for some people. The research shows that spiritual followers have less tendencies to social problems such as substance abuse, promiscuity, gambling, etc. Religious people tend to have a larger view on life, an existential thinking which provides some solace when facing hardship. However, in liberal environments, every aspect of life has to be curtailed and managed and regulated for the market, hence the attack on groups who are 'off-grid' or different, like communes, travellers, etc. Some groups are given privileged status whilst others are harassed and intimidated for their beliefs. Equanimity, an idea fought over for generations in Britain by working-class people, is now regulated by the liberal market. Likewise, Argyle in *The Psychology of Happiness*[4] shows that the old adage of 'making a difference' by doing work which is meaningful, social, and beneficial, increases exponentially job satisfaction. The modern world is awash with faceless call centres and factory work designed to increase the efficiency (work) of individuals. Liberal democratic capitalism, despite a modern polish, has not qualitatively improved the lives of homo sapiens; in fact, it has worsened social justice, poverty, and feelings of friendship in community. It alienates people and removes social responsibility. Contemplation, meditation, and self-reflection are increasingly impossible for modern man; all around, a cacophony of sounds, screams, cars, and aeroplanes remove the individual from his world and throw him back into the chaos at increasing frequency. Solace is sought through recreational drugs, as quiet reflection is abolished; a US-inspired cultural media infects us with the mindless Hollywood of garbage culture.

One of the catastrophic results of the Industrial Revolution was the removal of the majority of populations away from a natural form of living in close, family-based agricultural communities for the horrors of the dark satanic mill. This resulted in the debilitation, both physically and psychologically, of working-class people. The same process now extends in the globalisation of capital to the Orient; traditional happy rural populations are forced to relocate to cities to industrial factories. The extensive development trick is merely a way to populate the mills of globalisation. Stephen Cotgrove in *Catastrophe or Cornucopia* outlines the demise of human values:

'Individuals are not valued for what kind of people they are, but by what they have achieved. In place of personal bonds of kinship and community, modern societies substitute impersonal bureaucratic relationships, and the cash nexus of the market place...individuals become instruments of production at work which maximises output at the expense of satisfaction. And the speed of technological change leaves little time for reflection...we have paid a high price for material well-being.'[5]

A teacher once asked John Lennon what he wanted to be when he grew up. He replied... 'Happy.' He was told that was the wrong answer. From my travels in various countries, one curious fact has struck me again and again. It is that 'developed' nations are far less friendly than 'undeveloped nations'. The development brigades of the World Bank and IMF pursue policies of development. They do this, not to increase levels of happiness in the peripheral nations, but to prepare the groundwork for capital, to expose these markets for investment. Investment means a trajectory into market capitalism and the uprooting of people from traditional ways of life. Why are developed nations so unfriendly? Happiness was once measured by community, family relationships. This has been supplanted by economic growth as an indicator of happiness, GDP (Gross Domestic Product). The problem with consumption, on the other hand, as a marker for happiness, is that it needs constant realignment, new purchasing. It was Abraham Maslow who famously produced his hierarchy of needs. He stated that the first level of need is physiological. i.e. food, water, shelter. The second level is the need for social acceptance, group acceptance, self-esteem. The third level is that of spiritual attainment, self-growth, meaningful work. Brendan Behan's hierarchy was that you only need three things in life: a meal, someone to love you, and a good drink! The first level of needs has remained more or less constant throughout history. What has changed since Maslow produced his schemata is that technology has evolved to be used as a replacement for the natural fulfilment of needs. Therefore, we see the replacement of social needs and affection with electronic communications through television and social media.

Consumers also use consumerism to elicit these needs – fashion is a means to acceptability, the automobile to status. However, the greater concern is the fact that the second level of needs is now met by consumerism and technology. People are persuaded to buy things they don't need, things which will quickly become obsolete, the constant pressure to keep up with the 'Joneses' or the 'Mukherjees'. There is a common assumption that the 'market' creates everything; if there is a need, then the market will act to supply it. This was the classical economic view of the Adam Smith economists – the market as a neutral facilitator of good. This was expanded by the utilitarian ethos of those like Bentham and 'the greatest happiness of the greatest number', thereby utilitarianism embraced the culture of consumerism as it was a means to happiness (or so they thought.). However, recent research suggests that markets are 'created', designed by elites in the world of advertising (the success of advertising to introduce women to smoking was completely manufactured in the US). Ernest Braun in *Futile Progress –Technology's Empty Promise* explains that desires are created:

'The desires are those of the engineers and scientists, ambitious to achieve ever more elegant solutions to self-imposed problems. The desires are also those of the entrepreneurs, eager to carve out a niche for themselves and make a good profit. The desires are those of manufacturers, eager to stimulate new waves of purchases for new products when markets are saturated.'[6]

The best and clearest example is the US. Before mass consumerism took over the country, the prevailing ethos of the founding fathers – the people searching for a brave new world – believed in a philosophy of moderation, religion, and hard work. That same culture has now spiralled into one of greed and self-indulgence. The US realised quite quickly that a consumer culture in itself was not enough. There needed to be 'constant' consumerism, hence the rise of 'rapid obsolescence'; the incremental adaptation of technologies, goods into newer models – the next model of car, mobile phone, internet connection – an ever-expanding market. These products are not 'needs'; they are deliberately marketed and advertised to create markets. The invisible hand of the market has nothing to do with it. This is prevalent in all markets – high sugar content foods are highly marketed, with a promise of happiness if you drink Coke. This is not only immoral, but wastes the time and resources in manufacturing these products which could be put to better use. Individuals, as well as governments, are responsible. The culture in the UK is indicative of the malaise. Visit any UK city or town at the weekend and you see thousands and thousands of people weaving around shopping centres in a stressful pursuit of the next fashion, the next model, the next shopping high. Traditional pursuits such as walking, cycling, sports, are on the decline, but shopping is up. People in the UK associate higher incomes and consumerism to happiness. The bad news is that, despite increases in per capita wealth in industrialised nations, happiness has declined rapidly. Research into happiness comparisons is notoriously difficult, but there are general trends. It has been shown that some of the happiest people in the world are the Maasai in East Africa, Bangladeshis, and Nepalese. They share one thing in common – poverty, as they are continuously told by development agencies in shiny Land Rovers. Colonialism and the new globalisation are encroaching on these traditional values.

A very good example of the clear relationship between increasing materialism and depression is the case of the traditional Amish community in the US. In the middle of one of the world's largest consumer-obsessed countries, the Amish suffer a tenth of the cases of depression and suicide than their neighbours driving up and down shopping malls and eating in McDonalds. The attraction to material culture produces an endless cycle of desires and wants, which repeats ad infinitum. The psychological underpinning of diminishing returns from materialism is evident in the psychological theory of 'Hedonic Adaptation', whereby the gap between aspiration and achievement is a constant – in that the reaching of one aspiration then becomes the norm; hence the escalation of wants to another level, and so on. People who have suffered serious illness can often recognise the idiocy of this when they come out of hospital care, for example.

Allied with Hedonic Adaptation is Status Adaptation, whereby people consider that increasing their status in society through higher positions, etc, will give them satisfaction. Humans show their social position through elaborate gestures – one of them being status symbols. In pre-industrial societies this was unnecessary, because we lived in close proximity to our local group or tribe; people knew each other, and preposterous pretensions were quickly seen through. Even today, certain professions have a sense of higher social status, as there isn't the realisation in the division of labour that job titles really mean nothing; they are just titles. In the UK and US, the class system gives the illusion of totemic superiority to middle class 'white collar' professions. In essence, technology has facilitated the quick fix pursuit of happiness through material means. The technological consumer finds satisfaction in machines, in drugs (especially alcohol), television; they replace real satisfactions associated with nature, with harmony, with family, with community pursuits. The disconnectedness of individuals to each other has led to an extremely selfish and individual ethos amongst people in industrialised countries. Evidence has shown that people of materialistic bent are more likely to be aggressive, selfish, and alienated from personal relationships.

Tim Kasser in *The High Price of Materialism*[7] provides evidence that materialistic people suffer from high levels of alienation in relationships and community activities. Much happier are people who emphasise, by their work and hobbies, interests in autonomous and authentic experience. Far better is what Martin Seligman points out in *Authentic Happiness* when he talks about self-actualising, interesting activities. The more developed the nation, the more problems people have in the interface of society and happiness. Those old boring things such as gratitude, optimism, helping others, empathy, and self-analysis, are traits demeaned by a modern culture of self, of entitled rights. One huge source of conflict and alienation is the fact that lots of people subconsciously know they are doing jobs which are ethically wrong. However, they are thrown into a culture where even health-orientated and educational schema become part of a neo-liberal profit drive. The fundamental recourse is to recalibrate to authentic existence on both the level of individual beings and the superstructure of institutions, government. It is only through a synthesis of the two that human existence and community can be refound.

The Next Renaissance

Civilisation resembles the Icarian myth; Daedalus is the technological creator culture as it morphs its way, through accumulated knowledge, from agriculture to industry to technology. Icarus is the human heading towards the fulcrum, the sun. Progress and technology presumes that the sun can be reached, that it is, in fact, the 'solution' to contemporary issues, from poverty to environmental catastrophe. The hubris of civilisation is that the technological and accumulative elites will assure us of the possibility of flying too close to the sun. The majority of humankind, however, have little interest in technological fantasy. They are embroiled in a cyclical struggle for existence. The average existence of a species is approximately one million years. If we articulate that we have been on the planet for say 200,000 years, it is an act of outrageous hubris to go 'all in' on technology. The truth is that technology will not stop hunger and the marginalisation of the vast majority of the world's population. Technology aids and abets the accumulative elites of modernity. The way technologies are utilised is towards a tech-industrial schema to extend inequality and the abusive policies of states such as China. Technology has an inherent presumption of positivity, that the arc towards the sun is just one glorious road. There is no moral underpinning of the technological path; this is witnessed in the moral show-jumping amidst stem cell research, artificial semination, etc.

In the course of history's tech party weekend, the entire moral teleology of history has been abandoned by modernity. The Owl of Minerva has been caged, and whilst humanity has become more powerful, it has become less wise. However it might sound, this is not a call to Luddite profundity; on the contrary, it means a path like the Buddhist one at Borobudur. The huge Buddhist complex at Borobudur in Magelang, Java, consists of a labyrinthine complex of corridors and stairways, guided by the knowledge reliefs of 1400 panels throughout the journey. The reliefs encompass Kings, Queens, Commoners, Hermits, and Bodhisattvas. It is a spiritual, long, and learned path, not an Icarian leap. The path sees the pilgrim gracefully move towards truth and wisdom. Recent apocalyptic scenarios usually depict the dystopian world of nuclear war aftermath or existential threats destroying civilisation. The pressing contemporary concerns are even more urgent, and that means moral retrenchment, which is the precursor to solving the existential threats. Without a moral framework, consumerism, environment failures, and zoonotic pandemics will continue to fuel these threats. Fashionable modern philosophers sum up the obsessions of dislocated modernity; abortion of disabled children is justified on the grounds that the foetus has no rationality or autonomy. If we were to call the abortion of disabled people 'Eugenics' then we would be back in the realms of Nazi Germany. Again, language can frame any issue, however horrible it is. Infanticide, euthanasia, surrogacy, are all matters of what is called a utilitarian approach. These moral universalist approaches to scientism cloud any ethical, moral trajectory. They posit a type of know-all conformity, of liberal assurance of a linear, paternal world.

The need for a moral teleological response does not come from a merely ethical stance, as say within a Christian or Islamic outlook. Technology and its dangers have made a long-term moral outlook inevitable. For we are not only providing a framework for sons and daughters, but for thousands and thousands of years into the future. That teleology stretches into the future and comes from the past. It is only visible in the present. Existential and technological risk means that leading a virtuous life, away from the mores of the individual, the market, means 'shaping' technology, the State, and the environment. This approach needs a syncretic fusion of the individual, a virtuous state, and to reconstruct language from the debris of conventional terminology and pseudo-speak; the liberal penchant for 'right practice', 'democracy', 'rights', and so forth, which act like a confessional box through which people are forced to view the world. In fact, if we were to remove all language and start afresh, we would have to reconstruct a truth from the rubble; there would be no ability to frame, deceive, or manipulate.

Take, for example, the 'hard' question of consciousness. The scientist may be able to elicit everything about your brain, how it works, the neurons, the chemicals, etc. However, the scientist cannot deduce from that, that you see the colours and the sounds. Leibniz gave the example of the brain as a mill. Imagine that you could walk inside to see the parts clicking and moving together; you could not deduce, however, that there were a mind saying, 'I can experience this.' This is the hard problem of consciousness. There are aspects we only know because we experience them. There is a huge gap of what we don't know; what is consciousness, for example. Therefore, it is inadvisable to model things only on reason, or what we observe, or the utilitarian view of experience; the world is much more, both in the teleology of the past to the science of the future.

Political Philosophy was a discipline which grappled with ideas such as democracy, liberty, justice. The twentieth century, however, saw the rise of Political Science as a leading subject of study. Political Philosophy was seen, by some, as old-fashioned and Political Science instead focussed on empirical scientific study of subjects such as voting, public policy, citizenship, structures. It was a more 'quantitative' approach. However, Political Philosophy grapples with the need for the principles or justifications for regimes. So, we see in the contemporary world a fleeting, technical analysis of problems – that if we tweak with the apparatus, the solutions will come. As we have seen, it is rooted in an atomised individual, a lack of telos. It is clear that Political Science has failed in that sense, that underlying moral and ethical concerns, democratic principles, and ideas of 'how we should live' have been neglected. My contention is that they have been deliberately obscured by an academia and intelligentsia more concerned with compliance to ephemeral zeitgeists, fads, and funding, than substantive ideas; The twentieth century saw the attempt to reconcile liberty and equality, with philosophers such as John Rawls dividing up the spoils in a very modern way, but neglecting the formative, basic teleology of the past as influencing the present. Rawl's 'reflective equilibrium' – the balance between liberty and equality – is stated 'within' the liberal paradigm. The social contract – the hypothetical 'deal' between the governors and the governed, put forward by Rousseau – is in abeyance. Elites and technology have broken the social contract, for the governed are now bereft of liberty and justice. Consequently, a renaissance of revalued Political Philosophy is necessary, whereby the failure of the modern liberal experiment is accepted.

Political Science and liberal political philosophers such as Rawls saw reason above emotion. The political and moral life, therefore, becomes merely another section of science to be dissected. It was Nozick who questioned the notion of the big state, and asserted the libertarian rights of individuals in his *Anarchy, State and Utopia*; the State should merely be the 'night watchman' between capitalistic competition. Nozick was correct in seeing that these 'natural rights', which predated the idea of the Social Contract, came before institutions and government. However, Nozick's conception of individuals as in Kant's 'ends in themselves' overstretched the individualistic account and was a convenient attempt, used later, to justify ideas such as unfettered markets, privatisation, etc. Therefore, twentieth century political philosophy was a constant struggle between liberty and justice, but without recourse to an underlying schema of morality and ethics. The task now is to see that the two are, in fact, reconcilable, if a different conception of meaning and teleology is accepted. However, the teleology of Aristotle, his essentialism (as seeing an essential Platonic form to things), was not a theory of history. The teleology is one of recognising the moral virtue of an individual's development through symbiosis with correct structures of the State and the external world.

The moral telos is represented in modernity by references to taboos. These taboos are remnants of Christianity, Islam; old-fashioned sentiments which must be vanquished by the liberal in historical 'progress'. Therefore, the modern moral philosopher grapples with the leftovers (taboos) of classical thought, not really grasping them, as if in a vacuum. For they have lost their origin, their telos. Archaic societies had invested in them a telos or meaning, a clarity of assumptions. It was the fusion of morality and social structure which made Islam the force it is. In archaic society there was that purpose of fusion; people were defined as to what they did, and that was allied to real life. There was no conception of inner, atomised man. Modern man has lost the representation of this unified vision of life which simplified existence; it was cyclical and had meaning. Hence Alistair McIntyre's conception of 'Internal' and 'External' goods; the pursuit of internal goods conforms to the form of telos, and this means following careers, goals, which reveal ethical characters. External goods are concomitant with uncaring competition, corruption, nepotism, working for unethical companies. Acquisition and bureaucratic individuals have replaced authentic man. Therefore, an ethical life comes also from within homo sapiens; it is not the historicism imposed by material Communism or given by rights. Modern life has been atomised, divided, as in work-life balance, public-private. Alternatively, communities and groups draw people into a narrative of duty and giving, rather than rights. Consequently, the modern philosophical traditions (Rawls and Nozick) – although the former from a liberal equality mode and the latter from a libertarian economic mode – are not based on a moral underpinning. The remit in the new dark ages of atomised technological angst is to return to archaic community and teleology, and to reassemble the library of books which Liebowitz has salvaged from antiquity.

Camus's *The Plague* was a metaphor for a plague we all carry within ourselves, and one which springs forth whenever crisis emerges. Therefore, it is about the precarity of existence, and that the Plague is everywhere, in institutions, within capitalism, within socialism, within ourselves. The Plague cannot be vanquished, but we can make it better through everyday decency and recognising it in ourselves. It means questioning the assumptions given to us, trying to shape history in a good way, but accepting the limits of cyclical being. The essential falsity of liberal thinking is that the linear march of history means that all social problems, all injustices, all historical anomalies, will be ironed out as progress continues with the march of science. Young Europeans or Americans do not have living memories of catastrophic events in history; the post-World War 2 generations have been immune to existential threats. There lies the multiplied horror of Coronavirus. Modern homo sapiens are divorced from precariousness. Physics and reason will provide a solution to everything whilst, behind this deceit, is the fact that the Yellowstone Super volcano, for example, if erupted, has a strength a million times of the Hiroshima bombing. Modern liberals want solutions to everything; discomfort shall not be allowed. Catastrophe is something 'out there' for the periphery of the Third World – the people in flood areas, the inhabitants of Mosul, the victims of proxy technological war in Syria. The correct path is to accept the slings and arrows, to accept that existence is cruel and violent – in that is a form of Buddhist catharsis and solace. The media applauds the wasted energy of virtue signalling, of empathy sounding, of awareness trumpeting from the literati of *The New Yorker*, whilst society lurches forward aimlessly from crisis to crisis without leadership. Archaic, traditional man was able to abolish time, and accepted the rhythmic complexities of existence without the constant strain of linear progress. Traditional man did not depend on the exemplar of historical events. This type of archaic thinking continues to a large degree within agricultural societies. Consequently, agrarian, cyclical societies are often vehemently attacked by revolutionary or liberal ideology. Christianity tried to impose an historical line with the introduction of the idea of the 'Redemption', and there it floundered. It was Heidegger who showed that historicism gave no hope of transcending historical time.

There is a need for man to glimpse the transcendental value of life; without it, man cannot come to terms with events such as plagues and wars. The transcendental view questions notions of scientific progress as being material and historicist. In essence, we are not dependent on the present as something which merely passes us by, historical events. Heidegger believed that man could unite time – the ecstases of future, past, and present. In the modern epoch, the conception of time is the historical present defined by the media, the workplace. Heidegger's idea of resoluteness means that individuals can seize the present and create the present for themselves, irrespective of historical time. Politics and philosophy have treated man's relationship with the world in typical Cartesian terms: subject and object. History has been 'out there', inflicted on the individual. However, the meaning of authentic existence, in Heidegger's conception of 'dasein' (being) is the notion of unconcealment and the individual's real feeling of existing in the world. The question of being, like democracy, is not one which can be delegated. However, in inauthentic and technological existence, life is delegated... to work, to technology, to representation. The death of the Enlightenment means grasping back from this isolation. Eliades remarks on the problem of modern man's belief in the progress of history:

'It is becoming more and more doubtful...if modern man can make history. On the contrary, the more modern he becomes, that is without defences against the terror of history – the less chance he has of himself making history. For history either makes itself or it tends to be made by an increasingly smaller number of men who not only prohibit the mass of their contemporaries from directly or indirectly intervening in the history they are making (or which the small group are making), but in addition have at their disposal means sufficient to force each individual to endure, for his own part, the consequences of this history, that is, to live immediately and continuously in dread of history.'[1]

Therefore, man needs the ability, like in nature every spring, to renew himself, in perpetuity. Historical societies of the modern world preclude the ability to make freedom. But freedom is not something 'given' by government or institutions; it is akin to a natural state. What we have within modern occidental thinking is the destruction of the ability to create, to reinvent existence. We have been chained by institutions and gimmicks of progress which have removed 'freedom' and 'truth' from man's essential existence. In 1969, the year of the 'Hong Kong Flu' in the US which killed 200,000 people, no schools, no restaurants, or festivals such as Woodstock were cancelled. There was no cabal of media and government making history, imposing history on individuals.

We are at the point of a juncture, a seismic evaluation of values. We have seen how plague can hasten or effect massive social change; we saw this with the Plague of Justinian and the Bubonic Plague, which led to the collapse of feudalism. The media misrepresents history; they misrepresent the news because of a particular agenda or narrative. Division is essential for elites; to divide is to rule. The fragmentation of the working-class base is evident in identity fawning – an attempt to say that some groups are more important than others. This is a deliberate attempt to isolate working-class people. Traditional alliances with ethnic minorities have been jettisoned, not because the working-class are 'nativist' but because of elite manipulation. This is replicated within feminist accounts. Despite the lessons of history, there is a huge degree of intolerance from every side, from every movement. The liberal culture of dominance presides over every movement, from Antifa to feminism, to Proud Boys. I am right; you are wrong. Quiet, reflective people, with a sense of nuance, are left disenfranchised and alienated. In the middle of the Coronavirus pandemic, protesting groups pursue the agenda with a disrespect for others, especially older members of the community. The media have driven an agenda of black rights, of the historic abuse of slavery, regardless of the fact that Democrats in the US hold power in most of the states in turmoil, that Democrat Presidents such as Clinton and Obama have had a myriad of opportunities to address working-class poverty but never delivered. It substitutes a narrative of entitlement, of abstracted rights. A sense of giving, of community, of self-realisation and reform, are ignored. Irish indentured slaves, sent to the Caribbean, suffered appalling brutality at the hands of the colonial planters. However, that white people could experience a similar fate to African slaves does not fit a particular narrow narrative, and there is a constant media attempt to belittle the Irish forced emigration 'myth'. The Irish sent by Cromwell were term-bound, chattel property of the planters and, although this was not the life-long, heritable slavery of African slaves, such contractual niceties were not of much consolation to either group. There was no recourse to the Human Rights lawyer. They suffered shocking abuse, as outlined in Sean O'Callahan's *To Hell or Barbados – The Ethnic Cleansing of Ireland*. Slavery in Mali continued to 2015. African nations from Mali to Ghana have apologised for their role in the Slave Trade. In fact, it was moral conservatism, Wilberforce and white privilege, which abolished slavery.

The ideas behind liberal capitalism are presented in positive ways: individualism, mobility, social mobility, progress, and technological advancement. The use of language enables anything to be raised to the level of acceptable, but individualism, mobility, and technology take people away from family and community, and alienate individuals from their true self – the essence of being. Television, which was once seen as 'make believe' entertainment, has become a weapon of propaganda, inculcating a weak and passive populace. The average person in industrialised countries spends 4 to 5 hours watching television per day. A widely-held myth is that technology is autonomous and that humans have, at the end of the day, free will. However, technology takes people away from authentic experience, removes people from communal fulfilling activities, and leaves people staring and screaming, Munch-like, into computer screens. We are at a stage where we have little knowledge as yet of the real psychological damage and alienation which the Internet causes to young people, although 'The Social Dilemma' (2020) documentary by Jeff Orlowski, Davis Coombe, and Vickie Curtis, sheds light on surveillance capitalism, addiction, and adolescent suicide. The technological imperative means an unquestioning acceptance of technology, despite its problems. We have traded freedom for the consumption of a range of consumer products. We are told that industrialised farming is the only way to feed the increasing population. We are told that genetically modified crops are the way forward – but there is no discussion, no vote, no democracy about it. The more technology develops, the more we 'appear' to be dependent on it, and the more we lose the realm of freedom. The scientists who promote technology research are funded by grants from corporates and government departments (essentially a small group of senior civil servants); therefore, the technological imperative is a consumerist imperative which co-opts 'individuals' into the framework and away from community. There is no democratic mandate for the destruction of land through pesticides, or the destruction of the environment through synthetic chemicals. Technology and the concentration of wealth means that new technologies are designed for a wealthy elite consumer market rather than addressing the problems of the urban poor, simply because they have no purchasing power. In a Darwinian sense, only technologies which maximise profit will be utilised; a new technology can be seen like a genetic mutation – taken up by reason of being profitable. However, profitable does not mean socially useful. The organised nomenklatura of the technology elites means that corporations (PLCs) and limited companies can hide behind a legal form, i.e. a company. This is used to mask the source of unethical decisions or behaviour, and the corporates are only answerable to shareholders who want maximised profit. Darwin would have recognised that societies suffering from inertia and stagnation will fail in the Nietzschean struggle for survival; this will favour homogenous societies with a specialised executive class and a rigorous, pluralist separation of powers, a civil society of competent schools, universities, and institutions. Countries exposed to whims and the dumbing-down of expertise will lose out in the 'survival of the fittest'.

The nature of vested interests throughout society makes the switch to a better method of living unlikely through existing elites. The engrained selfishness of the economic and political elites, the bureaucrats in the EU, in national governments, the World Bank, in the IMF, will not change their *modus operandi*. Thomas Kuhn in *The Structure of Scientific Revolutions*[2] points out that scientific revolutions occur, not because of scientific elites but in spite of them, and usually later as the old thinkers die out. Therefore, we cannot rely on existing elites to recognise truths; for societal change we will need to rely on young people. However, they too suffer from the elites' control of social media, education, internet; they are 'tuned into' the new technologies, but are manipulated by them. The modern world method of globalisation is based on extraction – the removal of individuals from traditional structures and moral paradigms. The madness of this system of isolated individuals means that previous paradigms have been excluded. Religions which promised 'brotherhood', social movements which promised cooperation, are demonised. Indigenous peoples are marginalised and exploited, even though they are the only attempts at unification rather than separation. The move to a new society entails the abolition of growth, the removal of consumer culture, the devolution of centralised nation states. This will need to be replaced by steady state municipal economies, removed from corporations and states. The present unsustainable agricultural model needs a return to small homesteads and self-sufficiency.

When Neitzsche proclaimed that 'God is Dead' he foresaw homo sapiens as the prisoner without walls, the man, as Sartre had said, who was 'condemned to be free'. In this, 'freedom' is not a blessing but a curse. Freedom is only for the 'Superman' with the capacities of the 'will to power'. He had attempted to replace the Theistic God with the Superman and having stared into the abyss of a world without values, had invented the Superman. Having killed God and abandoned the Idols Neitzsche had called on man to 'become' a God. In 'Thus Sprake Zarathustra' he formalised the essence of the modern dilemma;

'You call yourself free? Let me hear your ruling thoughts, and not that you have escaped bondage. Are you one who deserved to escape from it. There are many who threw away their only worth when they threw away their servitude. Free from what? Why should Zarathustra care? Your eyes should answer plainly: free for what?'

In the post -existentialist Nihilism, the new men of modernity, chained in the desert wasteland, proclaim the ideas of rights, utility and materialism. They replace values, replace character. Man does not know how to act, how to use this freedom. The man in the desert wastes resembles the existential angst and horror of the 'Waste Land'. Modern men do not deserve freedom; the petty protesters of BLM haven't earned their freedom, they haven't contributed, developed the Aristotelian 'charakter'. As Dostoevsky had noted, once we had killed God, anything was permitted- a freedom without values. Being a God means duties and obligations, the telos of existence. Man is suspended on the webs he has created, stretched across an abyss - on the other side lies the Superman. To arrive there, through stormy waters, requires courage, truth and the eternal return to essences and the forms of tradition. Man is staring into the abyss, chained to the walls of Plato's cave whilst the light is dimming faster and faster. From the darkness, Coronavirus has, inadvertently, offered Homo Sapiens an opportunity to revalue the world, to walk out of Plato's cave, to be free..but for something.

INDEX

Appendix

INEQUALITY:

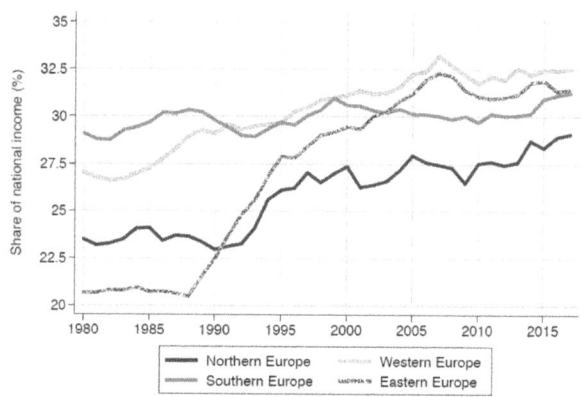

Source: authors' computations on the basis of household surveys, fiscal data and national accounts. WID.world/europe2019. Interpretation: between 1980 and 2017, the share of total income captured by the top 10% in the Eastern European countries rose on average from 20% to over 30%. Country averages weighted by adult population.

FDI:

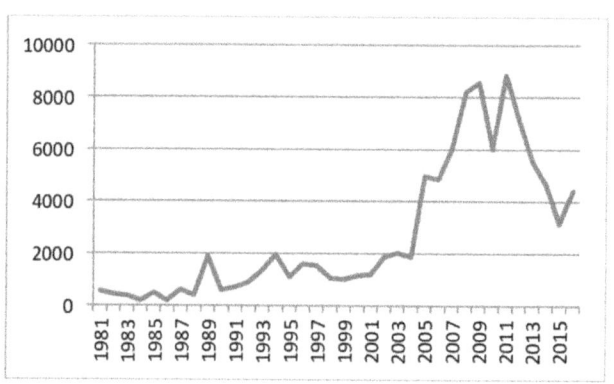

Bibliography

Alston, Philip. 'Statement on Visit to the United Kingdom', prepared by OHCHR (16 Nov, 2018). Accessed 18 November, 2019. https://www.ohchr.org/en/NewsEvents/Pages/DisplayNews. aspx?NewsID=23881&LangID=E

Argyle, M. (2009) *The Psychology of Happiness*. London: Routledge.

Aristotle, H. Rackham, and Stephen Watt. (1996) *The Nicomachean Ethics*. Ware, Hertfordshire: Wordsworth.

Bentley, Jerry H. (1993) *Old World Encounters: Cross-Cultural Contacts and Exchanges in Pre-Modern Times*. New York: Oxford University Press.

Bergen-Cico, Dessa & Scholl, Susan & Ivanashvili, Nato & Cico, Rachael. 'Opioid Prescription Drug Abuse and Its Relation to Heroin Trends.' (2016) 10.1016/B978-0-12-800213-1.00082-1

Bishop, B. & Cushing, R. G. (2009) *The Big Sort: Why the Clustering of Like-Minded America is Tearing Us Apart*. Boston, Mass: Mariner Books.

Bloom, P. (2010) 'The Moral Life of Babies.' *New York Times*. May 5, 2010. https://www.nytimes.com/2010/05/09/magazine/09babies-t.html

Braun, Ernest. (1995) *Futile Progress: Technology's Empty Promise*. London: Earthscan Publications.

Campbell, Denis. 'UK unprepared for Flu Epidemic'. *Guardian*, 2 Jan, 2014.

Chancel, Gethin, Blanchet. 'How Unequal is Europe? Evidence from Distributional National Accounts, 1980-2017', World Inequality Lab, 2019.

Chew, Sing C. (2007) *The Recurring Dark Ages: Ecological Stress, Climate Changes, and System Transformation*. Lanham: Altamira Press.

Cotgrove, Stephen. (1982) *Catastrophe or Cornucopia: the Environment, Politics and the Future*. Chichester: Wiley.

Craddock, S., Hinchliffe, S. (2015) 'One world, one health? Social science engagement with the one health agenda.' *Social Science & Medicine* Vol 129, 1-4.

Dambisa, Moyo. 'Why foreign aid is hurting Africa.' *The Wall Street Journal*. March 21, 2009. https://www.wsj.com/articles/SB123758895999200083

Diamond, Jared. (2019) *Guns, Germs and Steel: A Short History of Everybody for the Last 13,000 Years*. London: Vintage.

Diamond, Jared M. (2005) *Collapse: How Societies Choose to Fail or Survive*, London: Penguin.

Dawkins. R. *(1976) The Selfish Gene*. Oxford: Oxford University Press UK.

Eliades, Mircea. (1965) *The Myth of the Eternal Return*. New York: Pantheon Books.

Elster, J. (2016) *Sour Grapes: Studies in the Subversion of Rationality*. New York: Cambridge University Press.

FDI trends in BRI Economies. Accessed 3 March 2020. https://blogs.worldbank.org/trade/foreign-investment-growth-belt-and-road-economies

Ferrier, Simon & Ninan, K.N. & Leadley, P. & Alkemade, Rob & Acosta, L.A. & Akcakaya, H. Resit & Brotons, Lluís & Cheung, William & Christensen, Villy & Harhash, Khaled Allam & Kabubo-Mariara, Jane & Lundquist, Carolyn & Obersteiner, M. & Pereira, H. & Peterson, Garry & Pichs-Madruga, R. & Ravindranath, N. & Rondinini, Carlo & Wintle, B. 'Summary for policymakers of the methodological assessment of scenarios and models of biodiversity and ecosystem services of the

Intergovernmental Science-Policy Platform on Biodiversity and Ecosystem Services.' IPBES (2016)

Feuerbach, Ludwig Andreas. (1989) *The Essence of Christianity*. New York: Prometheus Books.

Frankopan, Peter. (2016) *The First Crusade: The Call from the East*. Cambridge, MA: Belknap Press of Harvard University Press.

Fukuyama, Francis, F. (1992) *The End of History and The Last Man. Francis Fukuyama*. New York: Perennial.

Graeber, David. (2011) *Debt: The First 5000 Years*, Brooklyn: Melville House Press.

Hamilton, C. (2021) *Hidden Hand: Exposing how the Chinese Communist Party is reshaping the world*. S.l.: OneWorld Publications.

Hawkes, N. 'Air pollution in UK: the public health problem that won't go away.' *BMJ*. 350 (May, 2015).

Heidegger, M., & Heidegger, M. (n.d.). *Being and Time*. San Francisco: Harper.

Heidegger, Martin, and William Lovitt. (2013) *The Question Concerning Technology, and Other Essays*. New York: Harper Perennial.

Heinberg, Richard. (2008) *The Party's Over: Oil, War and the Fate of Industrial Societies*. Gabriola Island: New Society Publishers.

Huesemann, Michael, and Joyce Huesemann. (2011) *Techno-Fix: Why Technology Won't Save Us or the Environment*. Gabriola Island, BC: New Society Publishers.

Hume, D., & Lindsay, A. D. (1962) *A Treatise of Human Nature*. London: J. M. Dent & Sons.

Hymowitz. K. 'The Great Teen Sex Decline.' https://ifstudies.org/ifs-admin/resources/the-great-teen-sex-decline-city-journal-copy.pdf

Kahneman, Daniel. (2015) *Thinking, Fast and Slow*. New York: Farrar, Straus and Giroux.

Karkee, R. & Comfort, J. (2016) 'NGOs, Foreign Aid, and Development in Nepal. *Frontiers in Public Health'*, 4.

Kasser, Tim. (2006) *The High Price of Materialism*. Cambridge, MA: MIT Press.

Kossoff, P. (1983) *Valiant heart: A Biography of Heinrich Heine*. New York u.a.: Cornwall.

Kuhn, Thomas S. (2015) *The Structure of Scientific Revolutions*. Chicago, IL: The University of Chicago Press.

Lasco, Gideon. 'Why are people who use illegal drugs demonized?' *Sapiens*. (28 August, 2019). https://www.sapiens.org/culture/drug-users-demonized/

Layard, Richard, and George Ward. (2020) *Can We Be Happier?: Evidence and Ethics*. UK: Pelican, an imprint of Penguin Books.

Lederberg, J. (2000) 'Infectious History.' *Science*. 288: 287–93.

Mann, Michael. (1997) 'Has Globalization Ended the Rise and Rise of the Nation-State?' *Review of International Political Economy* 4, no. 3 472-96. www.jstor.org/stable/4177235

Massachusetts, https://malegislature.gov/Laws/Constitution

Marcuse, H. (2017) Repressive Tolerance. *Political Elites in a Democracy*, 138-169. doi:10.4324/9781315126654-8

Matthews, A. (2011) 'Post-2013 EU Common Agricultural Policy, Trade and Development. A Review of Legislative Proposals' International centre for Trade and Development. Accessed 9 January 2020. http://www.ictsd.org/themes/agriculture/research/post-2013-eu-common-agricultural-policy-trade-and-development-a-review

Matthews, A. 'An updated look at the impact of the EU's Common Agricultural Policy on developing countries'. ResearchGate. 2014. Accessed on 9 January, 2020 https://www.researchgate.net/

publication/280600752_An_updated_look_at_the_impact_of_
the_EU's_Common_Agricultural_Policy_on_developing_
countries

McCarthy, Niall. 'Estonia has world's worst drug problem.' Accessed on 4 February at Statista. https://www.statista.com/ chart/2305/estonia-has-europes-worst-drug-problem/

McFarlane, R.A., Sleigh A.C., McMichael, A.J. (2013) 'Land-use change and emerging infectious disease on an island continent.' *International Journal of Environmental Research and Public Health* Vol 10, No 7, 2699–2719.

Macintyre, A. (1984) *After Virtue*. Notre Dame, IN: University of Notre Dame Press.

Moyo. D. (2009) 'Why foreign aid is hurting Africa.' *The Wall Street Journal*. March 21. https://www.wsj.com/articles/SB123 758895999200083

Nietzsche, Friedrich Wilhelm. (2006). Thus spoke Zarathustra : a book for all and none. Cambridge :Cambridge University Press.

Nissani, Moti. (1990) 'A Cognitive Reinterpretation of Stanley Milgram's Observations on Obedience to Authority.' *American Psychologist*. 45 (12): 1384–1385.

Norbert-Hodge. (1991) *Ancient Futures: Learning from Ladakh*. Sierra Club.

Ord, Toby. (2020) *Precipice*. London: Bloomsbury.

Oppenheim, Sara. (2001) 'Alternative Agriculture in Cuba'. *ESA Journal* October. https://www.researchgate.net/profile/Sara_ Oppenheim/publication/233809459_Alternative_Agriculture_in_ Cuba/links/0912f50bbbf5a14584000000/Alternative-Agriculture-in-Cuba.pdf

Piketty, Thomas and Goldhammer, Arthur. (2020) *Capital and Ideology*. Cambridge (Massachusetts): Harvard University Press.

Posner, Gerald L. (2020) *Pharma: Greed, Lies, and the Poisoning of America*. New York: Avid Reader Press.

Putnam, Robert D. (2000) *Bowling Alone*. New York: Simon & Schuster.

Quammen, David. (2012) *Spillover: Animal Infections and The Next Human Pandemic*. New York: W.W. Norton & Company.

Russell-Jones, Robin. (2015) 'Air pollution in the UK: better ways to solve the problem.' *BMJ*. 357.

Sanders, D.M., Todd, C., Chopra, M. (2015) 'Confronting Africa's health crisis: more of the same will not be enough.' *BMJ 331* (7519), 755–758.

Seligman, Martin E. P. (2011) *Authentic Happiness*. North Sydney, N.S.W.: William Heinemann.

Shelter. *'Briefing: In work, but out of a home.'* Accessed 1 February, 2020. https:// england.shelter.org.uk/__data/assets/pdf_file/0004/1545412/2018_07_19_Working_Homelessness_Briefing.pdf 2018.

Streeck, Wolfgang. (2017) *How Will Capitalism End?* S.l.: Verso Books.

Streeck, Wolfgang. (2014) 'The Politics of Public Debt.' Public Seminar. https://publicseminar.org/2014/02/the-politics-of-public-debt/

Tainter. Joseph A. (2017) *The Collapse of Complex Societies*. Cambridge, Cambridgeshire: Cambridge University Press.

Thornton, P.K. (2010) 'Livestock production: recent trends, future prospects.' *Philosophical Transactions of the Royal Society of London B: Biological Sciences* Vol 365, No 1554 2853-2867.

UN. 'Human Development Report.' Accessed 2 Feb, 2020. http:// hdr.undp.org/en/countries/profiles/GBR

UN. 'Transforming our World: The 2030 Agenda for Sustainable Development.' Accessed 3 February, 2020. https://sustainable development.un.org/post2015/transformingourworld/publication

University of Copenhagen. 'Biodiversity crisis is worse than climate change, experts say.' ScienceDaily. www.sciencedaily.com/releases/2012/01/120120010357.html (accessed April 24, 2020).

Voll, John Obert. (1994) 'Islam as a Special World-System.' *Journal of World History*, no. 5, 2. 213-226.

Walker, A. T. (2015) 'The Equality Act: Bad Policy that Poses Great Harms.' The Public Discourse. https://www.thepublicdiscourse.com/2015/07/15381/

Warneken, F., & Tomasello, M. (2009). 'Varieties of altruism in children and chimpanzees'. *Trends in Cognitive Sciences, 13*(9), 397-402. doi:10.1016/j.tics.2009.06.008

World Bank. https://data.worldbank.org/indicator/NY.GDP.PCAP.KD.ZG.

World Inequality Database. 'Top 10% income shares in European regions, 1980-2017.' Accessed 2 March, 2020. https://wid.world/europe2019/

Yanai, I., Lercher, M. J. (2016) 'Forty years of The Selfish Gene are not enough'. *Genome Biol,* 17, 39. https://doi.org/10.1186/s13059-016-0910-7

Feuerbach, Ludwig Andreas. (1989) *The Essence of Christianity.* New York: Prometheus Books.

Notes

1   Feuerbach, Ludwig Andreas. (1989) *The Essence of Christianity.* New York: Prometheus Books.

Chapter 1

1   Ferguson, N. Report 9: 'Impact of non-pharmaceutical interventions (NPSs) to reduce COVID-19 mortality and healthcare demand.' Imperial College, London.

2   Geertz, C. (2017) *The Interpretation of Cultures.* London: Basic Books.

3   Diamond, Jared M. (2019) *Guns, Germs and Steel: A Short History of Everybody for the Last 13,000 Years.* London: Vintage.

Chapter 4

1   David Quammen. (2012) *Spillover: Animal Infections and The Next Human Pandemic.* New York: W.W. Norton & Company.

2   'Transforming our World: The 2030 Agenda for Sustainable Development', prepared by UN (New York), NY, 2015.

3   P.K. Thornton. (2010) 'Livestock production: recent trends, future prospects', *Philosophical Transactions of the Royal Society of London B: Biological Sciences.* Vol 365, No 1554, 2853–2867.

4   R.A. McFarlane, A.C. Sleigh, A.J. McMichael. (2013) 'Land-use change and emerging infectious disease on an island continent.' *International Journal of Environmental Research and Public Health,* Vol 10, No 7, 2699–2719.

5   Craddock, S., Hinchliffe, S. (2015) 'One world, one health? Social science engagement with the one health agenda.' *Social Science & Medicine,* Vol 129, 1-4.

Chapter 5

1   Chew, Sing C. (2007) *The Recurring Dark Ages: Ecological Stress, Climate Changes, and System Transformation.* Lanham: Altamira Press.

Chapter 6

1 Diamond, J. (2013) *Collapse: How Societies Choose to Fail or Survive*. London: Penguin.
2 Robin Russell-Jones. (2015) 'Air pollution in the UK: better ways to solve the problem.' *BMJ*. 357.
3 N. Hawkes. 'Air pollution in UK: the public health problem that won't go away.' *BMJ*. 350 (22 May, 2015).
4 Joseph A. Tainter. (2017) *The Collapse of Complex Societies*. Cambridge, Cambridgeshire: Cambridge University Press.
5 Toby Ord. (2020) *Precipice*. London, Bloomsbury.

Chapter 8

1 Aristotle, H. Rackham, and Stephen Watt. (1996) *The Nicomachean Ethics*. Ware, Hertfordshire: Wordsworth.
2 Jared Diamond, (2005 and 2011) *Collapse: How Societies Choose to Fail or Survive*. Penguin Books.
3 Rajendra Karkee & Jude Comfort. (2016) 'NGOs, Foreign Aid, and Development in Nepal.' *Frontiers in Public Health*. 4. 10.3389/fpubh.2016.00177.
4 Norbert-Hodge. (1991) *Ancient Futures: Learning from Ladakh*. Sierra Club.
5 University of Copenhagen. 'Biodiversity crisis is worse than climate change, experts say.' ScienceDaily. www.sciencedaily.com/releases/2012/01/120120010357.htm (accessed April 24, 2020)
6 Ferrier, Simon & Ninan, K.N. & Leadley, P. & Alkemade, Rob & Acosta, L.A. & Akcakaya, H. Resit & Brotons, Lluís & Cheung, William & Christensen, Villy & Harhash, Khaled Allam & Kabubo-Mariara, Jane & Lundquist, Carolyn & Obersteiner, M. & Pereira, H. & Peterson, Garry & Pichs-Madruga, R. & Ravindranath, N. & Rondinini, Carlo & Wintle, B. (2016) Summary for policymakers of the methodological assessment of scenarios and models of biodiversity and ecosystem services of the Intergovernmental Science-Policy Platform on Biodiversity and Ecosystem Services. IPBES.
7 Huesemann, Michael, and Joyce Huesemann. (2011) *Techno-Fix: Why Technology Won't Save Us or the Environment*. Gabriola Island, BC: New Society Publishers.

8   Heinberg, Richard. (2008) *The Party's over: Oil, War and the Fate of Industrial Societies*. Gabriola Island: New Society Publishers.

9   Dukes, J.S. (2003) Burning Buried Sunshine: Human Consumption of Ancient Solar Energy. *Climatic Change* 61, 31-44. https://doi.org/10.1023/A:1026391317686

10 Hymowitz. K. 'The Great Teen Sex Decline.' https://ifstudies.org/ifs-admin/resources/the-great-teen-sex-decline-city-journal-copy.pdf

Chapter 9

1   Denis Campbell. 'UK unprepared for Flu Epidemic.' *Guardian* (2 Jan, 2014).

2   Kahneman, Daniel. (2015) *Thinking, Fast and Slow*. New York: Farrar, Straus and Giroux.

Chapter 10

1   World Bank. https://data.worldbank.org/indicator/NY.GDP.PCAP.KD.ZG.

2   Massachusetts. https://malegislature.gov/Laws/Constitution

Chapter 11

1   Wolfgang Streeck. (2017) *How Will Capitalism End?* S.l.: Verso Books.

2   Wolfgang Streeck. 'The Politics of Public Debt.' Public Seminar 2014. https://publicseminar.org/2014/02/the-politics-of-public-debt/

3   Dale, G., Holmes, C., & Markantōnatou, M. (2019). *Karl Polanyi's political and economic thought: A critical guide*. Newcastle upon Tyne: Agenda Publishing.

4   Thomas Piketty and Arthur Goldhammer. (2020) *Capital and Ideology*. Cambridge (Massachusetts): Harvard University Press.

5   Chancel, Gethin, Blanchet. 'How Unequal is Europe? Evidence from Distributional National Accounts, 1980-2017.' World Inequality Lab, 2019.

6   Statement on Visit to the United Kingdom, 16 Nov, 2018, prepared by OHCHR (16 Nov, 2018).

7 D.M Sanders, C. Todd, M. Chopra. 'Confronting Africa's health crisis: more of the same will not be enough'. *BMJ (2015) 331*(7519), 755–758.

Chapter 12

1 Kossoff, P. (1983) *Valiant heart: A biography of Heinrich Heine.* New York u.a.: Cornwall.

2 Kant, I. (2020) *Critique of Pure Reason.* S.l.: Outlook Verlag.

3 Dawkins, R. (1976) *The Selfish Gene.* Oxford, Oxford University Press UK.

4 Yanai, I., Lercher, M.J. (2016) 'Forty years of *The Selfish Gene* are not enough.' *Genome Biol* 17, 39. https://doi.org/10.1186/s13059-016-0910-7

5 Fukuyama, Francis, F. (1992). *The End of History and The Last Man.* New York: Perennial.

6 Dawkins, R. (1976) *The Selfish Gene.*, Oxford, Oxford University Press UK.

7 Bloom. P. (2010) 'The Moral Life of Babies.' *New York Times.* May 5, 2010. https://www.nytimes.com/2010/05/09/magazine/09babies-t.html

8 Warneken, F., & Tomasello, M. (2009) Varieties of altruism in children and chimpanzees. *Trends in Cognitive Sciences, 13*(9), 397-402. doi:10.1016/j.tics.2009.06.008

9 Hume, D., & Lindsay, A.D. (1962) *A Treatise of human nature.* London: J. M. Dent & Sons.

10 Nissani, Moti. (1990) 'A Cognitive Reinterpretation of Stanley Milgram's Observations on Obedience to Authority.' *American Psychologist.* 45 (12): 1384-1385.

Chapter 13

1 Marcuse, H. (2017) Repressive Tolerance. *Political Elites in a Democracy,* 138-169. doi:10.4324/9781315126654-8

Chapter 14

1 Graeber, David. (2011) *Debt: The First 5000 Years,* Brooklyn: Melville House Press.

2   Example adapted from: Kahneman, D. (2015) *Thinking, fast and slow*. New York: Farrar, Straus and Giroux.

3   Elster, J. (2016) *Sour grapes: Studies in the subversion of rationality*. New York: Cambridge University Press.

4   Adorno, T.W., & Horkheimer, M. (2016) *Dialectic of Enlightenment*. London: Verso Books.

Chapter 15

1   Mann, Michael. 'Has Globalization Ended the Rise and Rise of the Nation-State?' *Review of International Political Economy* 4, no. 3 (1997): 472-96. www.jstor.org/stable/4177235.

2   FDI trends in BRI Economies. (2018) https://blogs.worldbank.org/trade/foreign-investment-growth-belt-and-road-economies

3   Hamilton, C. (2021) *Hidden Hand: Exposing how the Chinese Communist Party is reshaping the world*. S.l.: Oneworld Communications.

4   Bishop, B., & Cushing, R. G. (2009) *The big sort: Why the clustering of like-minded America is tearing us apart*. Boston, Mass: Mariner Books.

Chapter 16

1   McWhorter, J. H. (2007) *Winning the race: Beyond the crisis in Black America*. New York: Gotham Books.

Chapter 17

1   Macintyre, A. (1984) *After Virtue*. Notre Dame, IN: University of Notre Dame Press.

Chapter 18

1   Mircea Eliades. (1965) *The Myth of the Eternal Return*. New York: Pantheon Books.

Chapter 19

1   Sara Oppenheim. 'Alternative Agriculture in Cuba'. *ESA Journal* October (2001). https://www.researchgate.net/profile/Sara_ Oppenheim/publication/233809459_Alternative_Agriculture_in_ Cub a/links/0912f50bbbf5a14584000000/Alternative-Agriculture-in-Cuba.pdf

Chapter 20

1   Seligman, Martin E. P. (2011) *Authentic Happiness*. North Sydney, N.S.W.: William Heinemann.

2   Putnam, Robert D. (2000) *Bowling Alone*. New York: Simon & Schuster.

3   Layard, Richard, and George Ward. (2020) *Can We Be Happier?: Evidence and Ethics*. UK: Pelican, an imprint of Penguin Books.

4   Argyle, M. (2009). *The Psychology of Happiness*. London: Routledge.

5   Cotgrove, Stephen. (1982) *Catastrophe or Cornucopia: The Environment, Politics and the Future*. Chichester: Wiley.

6   Braun, Ernest. (1995) *Futile Progress: Technology's Empty Promise*. London: Earthscan Publications.

7   Kasser, Tim. (2006) *The High Price of Materialism*. Cambridge, MA: MIT Press.

Chapter 21

1   Mircea Eliades. (1965) *The Myth of the Eternal Return*. New York: Pantheon Books.

2   Kuhn, Thomas S. (2015) *The Structure of Scientific Revolutions*. Chicago, IL: The University of Chicago Press.

Lightning Source UK Ltd.
Milton Keynes UK
UKHW041207230821
389329UK00001B/61

9 781839 756221